FROM THE LOST LETTERS
SENT - BOOK ONE: 1985 - 1992

FROM THE LOST LETTERS SENT - BOOK ONE: 1985 - 1992

Memoirs Of An Invisible Songwriter

LORD CHESTER L. BALDWIN II

A Lord Baldwin Happening

Contents

I

FROM THE LOST LETTERS SENT

Memoirs From An Invisible Songwriter

Book One: 1985 - 1992

LORD BALDWIN

(LORD CHESTER L. BALDWIN II)

2

Author's Notes:

FROM THE LOST LETTERS SENT

BOOK ONE - 1985 - 1992

What we have here is the FIRST book (of four) that documents the lyrics and memoirs of the first 44 albums of Lord Baldwin, (Lord Chester L. Baldwin II). These 44 albums, categorized as the "Archive Series," were recorded during the, "Analog" era. The varied recordings were accomplished using a TASCAM 4-track Cassette Recorder. Book ONE, represents the recordings of songs from 1985 to the middle of 1992,... represented in the first nine albums of the Analog era;

* 01 - Lonely Too Long *
* 02 - A Working Man *
* 03 - Forever Friends *
* 04 - Something Must Be Wrong *
* 05 - It Wasn't My Fault *
* 06 - On The Open Range *
* 07 - Taking Me For A Ride *
* 08 - Ever On *
* 09 - Spinning My Wheels *

Honesty, I rarely take the time to read what the preface tries to relate, or what is in the introduction, or to delve into the message that the author has presented because I want to just get to the book itself, and instead, knowing my probable audience to be my own family and close friends, this is a chance to let everyone know where my head was at when I started this magnificent journey into the vast domains of music and poetry, coloured by my all-encompassing experiences, good and bad and my particular philosophies of life and love; all in an effort to help you, the reader, be able to put together a picture of what it was that Lord Baldwin was trying to accomplish.

Please note as you are about to peruse the contents of this work before you; **From The Lost Letters Sent** that it can be broken up into three major parts of interest;

First, **the album cover art**, which, as noted previously, I'm delighted with, because I had such fun designing and creating them (as an icon if you will), to represent the songs, the music, the lyrics and poetry of that particular album.

Second, **the words, the lyrics, the poetry** – These "Words For Songs" come to me in my daily doings, when I'm riding my bike, when I'm trying to go to sleep and sometimes they come to me in my dreams. Sometimes playing my guitar invites the words for songs to come out and play. Sometimes I take an interest in a happening that needed documentation, even if it is just lyrics to a song. Sometimes I am driven by the administering of injustice and inequity to the down-home folks that have to deal with prejudice and discrimination just to live a life here in America, and I am driven to write a poem to reflect the way I am feeling at that time. I believe in the potential of each song being important, in part from its individual contribution and to its possibilities as a whole especially if it is a concept album. For that sometime in the future.

Third, we have the, "**Memoirs From An Invisible Songwriter**" which in and of itself is broken down into two parts; **One**; a collection of **stories** that may, or may not relate to the writings of the words for songs, and, **Two**; the **documentations of past happenings**, to give life to and clarify particular happenings, shed light on projects, explaining where I was, and what was happening at that time in my life, and then perhaps why it was that I felt the need to write the words I did, explain the challenges, the triumphs and failures, and reasonings, and decisions to the song's creation.

As I was originally putting this document together in 2001 as a project I was doing at The Evergreen State College, some of the stories and antidotes, fresh at the time, made a lot of sense so I kept them included. Besides being fun diversions to the whole, I believe the stories to be essential to help you gain a more balanced understanding, and it was my hope that some of the stories could shed light on who I was, what I was doing, my motivations and what it was that shaped me to go in the directions I did and why I did not go in other directions when the opportunities presented themselves. Regrettably, there was always so much more to include, but I needed to keep moving to get this work out and so, what you have here is not complete, nor do I think it ever will be. It is a work in progress though, and I reserve the right to revise, renew, renovate and or bring the "**Memoirs**" and "**Stories**" up to date.

As Lord Baldwin's music is now streaming worldwide, this book may act as a companion guide for the listener of Lord Baldwin's material, and for those who might be interested in what thought-processes and insights that Lord Baldwin was going through or was influenced by, along with stories that may be related to the creative processes.

PERHAPS SOME BACKGROUND

House on Margaret Street – Iron Mountain Michigan

In the mid-50s, my family was living in Iron Mountain Michigan where I was influenced early on to what music was all about and listening to the birth of Rock and Roll in my older brother John's bedroom. After my brother David, John's favorite brother, left in 1958, I was delegated to try to fill the gap that David's departure left, and so, while John and I would sit on his bed playing a variety of card games, we would be listening to music on his Westinghouse Tube Radio. From fan magazines of that era, like; "**Teen**" and "**Hep Cats**" and "**Dig**" and "**Rock and Roll Songs**" (a few of the titles that John collected along with his "**MAD**" magazines), John was well read and seemed to know everything about the artists that we were listening to, and he loved to share that information, telling me narratives and stories about his favorites; Elvis Presley, Ricky Nelson, Chuck Berry, Bill Haley and the Comets, the Platters, Fats Domino, Gene Vincent, Little Richard, the Diamonds, Pat Boone, the Everly Brothers, the Coasters, Sam Cooke, Jerry Lee Lewis, Tommy Edwards, Conway Twitty, Connie Francis, Jackie Wilson and Buddy Holley. My love for the music only grew even after John went into the navy in 1960.

When John left to go in the Navy, he asked me to watch over his stuff while he was gone and he entrusted me with his radio and his magazine collection. I put his radio on the dresser that I shared with my brother Richie and stored John's magazines in a broken wicker hamper in my closet along with my own prized comic books, and then, for safe keeping, I covered the pile with a tattered WWII parachute.

Sadly, maybe six months later, my mother grabbed us kids and ran away (for the second time) from her abusive

husband, (we'll just call him; Senior). There was very little time to prepare for the departure and we would be traveling light by Grey-hound bus with no space to take wanted possessions; only a change of clothes. I thought that we would be returning after their reconciliation, so I felt all my prized-good stuff was safe. And even years later, knowing the house on Margaret Street had been sold and others were now living there, I felt that I'd be able to go back to that house in Iron Mountain and go into that closet and retrieve all those treasures. That of course, never happened.

Early on, I found joy in expressing myself and feelings through artistic activities. At Glendora High School in 1967, I was really good at **making small clay caricature-bust sculptures**, like of hippies and such, and so desirable were these busts that, as they would come out of the kiln and be put on a shelf to cool, many of them disappeared before I got back to class to collect them. It is my hope that they still exist out there stoically sitting on mantlepieces in former student's homes or resting comfortably on top of someone's piano somewhere.

It was also during this time that, after submitting short stories and poetry to my English Teacher, Mrs. Ulrich, I was told by her that I had a gift of finding and expressing feelings through words. I let her know that the poetry I was writing was actually lyrics that I created to go along with the tunes that I had in my head, and she marveled even more when I told her that I did not have any instruments at home to work with the tunes in my head. She entered some of my poetry and two short stories in varied contests and circulating magazines and facilities that put out monthly publications. Meanwhile, as I was encouraged to continue writing poetry (and lyrics), and the positive reinforcements that I was a good writer, stirred me on to write even more. Unfortunately, my mother, after being physically abused yet again by her then husband, Senior, suddenly uprooted us to get away from Senior, and covertly, we took a cross-country route by train from Los Angeles and arrived in New York City by New Year's Eve 1967. I never found out anything about my material or if any of it ever did get published.

In the Pemberton Township High School in New Jersey, I had a great interest in **ink artwork using India ink** and a fine-tip calligraphy pen and afterwards, filling in the drawings using multi-coloured inks. It was like I created a page in a colouring book and then used inks to colour the pages. I had drawings hung on the walls of the school as well as in our home in Browns Mills. Sadly, when I left New Jersey none of my art went with me, and I hope that out of the dozens of drawings created at that time, some may have survived. It was also at Pemberton Township High School that I continued writing lyrics disguised as poetry chasing that dream that I would be a songwriter. To me, this was never the "impossible" dream because even early on, I believed in what I was attempting to do. And although, besides my harmonica, I had no musical outlet; no guitar or skills to play one, no piano to plunk out the creative endeavors to go along with my words, I felt the universe was calling out, saying. "What are you waiting for?"

In the late spring of 1971, I was accompanying my brother Richie who was driving to "The Pines Resort Hotel" in Fallsburg, New York; located in the Catskills. We were there to go to a concert, arguably I do not remember who it was; I think it was T. Rex ("Bang a Gong (Get It On)") or Emerson, Lake & Palmer. Anyway, not important.

We decided to get there early because the seating in those days was FCFS and we wanted to be up front. We arbitrarily arrived two hours early with absolutely no other cars or people there. We went into the facility and found it was totally deserted, but there, up on a short-rise stage, was all the band's instruments and equipment including a "Rickenbacker 325 Rose Morris Fireglo" guitar, kind of like the one John Lennon (the Beatles) and John Fogerty (Credence Clearwater Revival) played. I picked it up from its stand, sat on the edge of the stage and played the three or four chords that I knew. Even with my amateurship and even without it being plugged in, the guitar sang like out and resonated wonderfully.

I will admit that the influence of Satan was strong; I was sorely tempted, and in my head I knew that this iconic Rickenbacker 325 Rose Morris Fireglo guitar could very easily be mine. But also, in my head and moreover in my heart, I knew this Rickenbacker guitar was not mine, and that whoever owned this guitar would be very sad to have someone steal it. I said a prayer for strength and after motioning to my brother Richie, I immediately left the building to avoid taking the Rickenbacker guitar.

On the drive home the spirit confirmed to me that because of that one small act of honesty and integrity, that I would be blessed to be able to magnify that marvelous musical talent that I knew was inside me, just waiting for me to tap into; waiting to be more fully discovered. It also came to me, that had I taken the Rickenbacker, my musical talents would have been stifled, maybe even taken from me. I felt a glowing goodness inside me all the way back to our Bungalow at Spanners in Monticello NY, and that good feeling has continued to be with me ever since.

At the end of the summer of 1971, in Woodstock New York, I bought my first guitar; a **Yamaha 12-string** with a artificial alligator-skin, hard-shell case for two hundred and fifty dollars. I ditched the idea of getting a Guild 12 string (like the one John Denver had on the cover of, "Poems Prayers and Promises"), because, at the time, it was going for around $799.99 which was way beyond my price range. Right after that, with my friends Harvey and Lesa, (and their dog), I went on a road trip across the U.S. to get back to the west coast. Admittedly, I knew nothing about loosening the strings and relieving the tension on the neck and bridge of the guitar, that was packed and sitting up in the back window of the car. Through the corn country of Nebraska and Iowa, the sun, beating directly down on the guitar within the case, ended up cooking and warping the guitar neck. A month later, after newly arriving in Portland Oregon, the Yamaha guitar and the fake alligator hard-shell case was stolen from my apartment; probably (and sadly) by an acquaintance or pseudo friend. I was then down to going to the Portland State University music wing (third floor?) where there was a huge bank of semi-sound-proof piano rooms to practice in, as time would allow.

Okay, okay, getting off track here. It is obvious that I don't know what to say here or how to say it. Maybe you're asking yourself, why should I care about this book? What is so special about it, and who is this self-proclaimed Lord Baldwin? Maybe this Author's Note might sound better if it was presented from the third-person perspective or point of view, kind of like an outsider looking in? Let's try that out and see.

Many aspire to do great things, especially when they recognize that they've been entrusted with particular talents and gifts. It takes time and soul searching to discover the potential of those gifts but even from the beginning of the process, some begin to sculpture and to feed and to modify and to nurture their special dreams that they might grow into that distinct singular vision of that one day, where they will shine and be able to bask in their own bright **Starlight**.

What happens when that dream that we have been working with for so long, continues to be three or four steps in front of us? What if we can even visualize the dream and see it in motion with others that are moving about, wearing that dream; our dream, meanwhile, that same dream for us continues to be beyond our reach? Well, in spite of all the discouraging voices steeped in negativity to slow us down or turn us away, we have to choose to listen to our heart. I had to continue to plod on; I was after all, *on a mission*.

Never mind the great ones out there on center stage. Never mind the critics that pan your work and criticize your ineptness. And never mind the time it takes to complete that one simple expression of words and music that, arguably pales in the light of the accomplished, professional others. I was on a mission to find my words and my voice and my chord progressions and pursuing my vision of what I wanted others to know me by.

Us dreamers must continue to move forward. and in doing so, knowing that things too easily gained are too little esteemed, we keep chasing that dream, no matter how far in front of us it gets. We can't give up; we refuse to give up. We know that if we want this thing to work, we've got to believe.

And so, as we dreamers live and create and do what we feel we must, maybe with the hope that someday we will be noticed and our work, to be validated, we work in a void. A void where we see and hear them but they can't see us. And arguably if and when they do, their dull, arduously obligatory returned look seems to say, "it is so hard for me to tolerate your struggling ineptness." But they, the critics ,seem to come and go quickly and when we eventually get past the nursing of our own broken hearts and egos, we have to know that that recognition, good or bad, can't be our driving motivation,... not only because it'll only hurt that much more when it doesn't happen the way our dream had imagined, but as we are living in the new-normal, apathetic world of indifferent people, whose lack of concern for others, or lack of interest in anything that is not quickly self-serving, we have seen the likes of them and we decided in the beginning that we don't want to be one of those guys.

Eventually we the dreamers look to come to the understanding that in our long and colourful journey, illuminated by the *learning-from-our-mistakes* travels, we are there, in our own world, doing that thing that we love; we are there creating little masterpieces that, if not to anyone else, still have intrinsic values to us,... and to that end, we are kind of living some of the best parts of that dream,... and we begin to marvel in what we can do and we know that we have to continue to believe in our dream.

As this book may be read on a computer monitor or through a phone, illuminating your display of the pages, it is good to know that the book also includes all of the nine album's cover art in full colour representations. There are also liner notes about the covers included on the back pages of the album art itself, explaining some of the reasoning for Lord Baldwin's art designs; each an esoteric work of computer art and worthy of being displayed on good-quality, long-sleeve tee-shirts;... you know, the ones with at least three or four buttons in front like the ones that were sold in head shops in 1968?

Lastly,... I want to give thanks to the people and companies that without their product and services, I could not have presented such a package as you now have before you.

I want to thank Microsoft Office for the tools they included in their software packages that allowed me to document and manipulate all of my Microsoft Word writings, my Microsoft Excel spreadsheets, my Microsoft Access databases and my Microsoft Outlook correspondences to put things together. Also, all my finished album cover artwork was done with the sub-programs included in Microsoft Word, like WordArt and the, Pictures manipulation program.

I want to thank the free, open-source, GNU Image Manipulation Program, (GIMP 2.10.8) of which I have come to love, although, I have barely scratched the surface of what this free, Adobe Photoshop - Photo & Design like software can do, but it has saved me at least, $599.88 or the guilt I might have felt had I tried to pirate the Adobe software. Well done folks, well done indeed.

Big special thanks to my son Brian's best friend, (and my friend) Jamie Stanger who volunteered to work on my web page and is in the process of getting my web page, **(www.LordBaldwin.com)** up to date, in spite of the fact that he's fairly recently newly married to Jenna, they have a little 18-month-old boy, he has a new job and has had to move near two hours away to be closer to his work. Still, this web page is very important to me as the possible face and liaisons to the Lord Baldwin Happenings. Jamie and Jenna continue to be inspirational and positive, with upbeat ideas and encouraging suggestions to make the Lord Baldwin web pages better.

I want to thank Florian Heidenreich, an Indie Software Developer living in Dresden with a background in professional software development for over twenty years, for his "MP3TAG" free software, of which I am so humbly grateful to for the digital tagging of all my Wav and MP3 files, (songs). Over the years I have come to think of Florian as a good friend who has been with me on my journey, helping me to accomplish great things through his simple but magnificent program. Again, well done indeed.

Thanks to the people at "https://combinepdf.com/" who's free online software helped me to manipulate and combine my varied PDF files. They also saved me from the guilt I would have felt, had I pirated that Adobe software, also because of their free online service, I didn't have to pay $449.00 to the Adobe people for their Acrobat Pro software. Thank you, "CombinePDF.com."

I now wish to thank the very excellent people at DistroKid who helped me to get my music and song distributed and out throughout the world. I can't begin to express how grateful I am to finally have a chair to the world stage, and in spite of the number's rollercoaster of listeners, to have the ability to have people in Korea and Germany and India and Brazil and Norway and Japan and Australia and the United Kingdom be able to stream my material at any time and any place through Spotify and other streaming facilities is just so awesome. Thank you again folks so much for everything you've done for me. You guys rock!

As you can imagine, there are many other unsung heroes out there that I want to thank them for their help in making this new endeavor possible right now. And here is the shout out to my lovely best friend, Diane who unconditionally loves me and continues to believe in me, and inspires me to write the many love songs for her that she so richly and honorably deserves.

And here is my call out to all my children and their children. Please know that I dedicate all of this thing I do to all of you and again, to Diane, with my most sincere love and devotion,... I hope whomever you are, that you can find enjoyment in these pages of this documentation of these first nine albums along with the corresponding songs.

Yours Indubitably,
Lord Baldwin

3

SPECIAL NOTE TO MY FAMILY

I decided that I'd like to say something special, just to you; my children and to my children's children, (my grandchildren), so here goes. You all know me and know that I love music. It fills me up with happiness and can help me get out of bad places like when I'm feeling annoyed or angry about something. Music has healing powers that can mend your soul and repair your broken heart. I want you to know that music can have the same medicinal powers on you too, if you wish,... and you may or may not have pondered about this thought, but I want to address this here and now. There are things in our being that were passed on from generation to generation through our DNA. Things passed on from our mothers and from our fathers that help define the attributes that comprise our physical and chemical makeup. New scientific studies now suggest that some of our memories, fears, and behaviors are passed down genetically through generations from our ancestors. Recent studies done by epigenetic scientists and researchers even suggest that we receive loads of genetic memories from our parents, grandparents, and further ancestors, in an instinctive effort by their DNA to better prepare ours for difficult experiences that they have faced, such as fear, disease, or trauma. These epigenetic scientists also study how genes are inherited and the changes to those genetics that we exhibit, even when those changes are not essential to our DNA. These changes can be affected or recalled by our experiences, age, environment, and health.

It came to me one night a couple of months ago that within this receiving of coded genetic DNA that we were all given, through the transferal of genes from our fathers, mothers, grandmothers, grandfathers, etc., we also received special gifts and talents that we, if we so discover, could use and magnify. Let me be even more plain on this; our Heavenly Father has instilled within us, many gifts and talents, expecting us to discover them and to magnify those talents to accomplish great things while here on this earth. I believe that examining our heritage can help us to identify some of those gifts and talents. I don't have too much documentation to extrapolate data from the past because I only vaguely knew my great grandmother Viola Snook, on my mother's side, who, played harmonica in her teens in a band in 1885 and continued playing her whole life till her passing in 1970, but I can say with a certainty that both my grandparents on my mother's side, my mother, who played piano, and my father, who played accordion, organ and piano, all inherited and used their special gift of music. Some of our ancestors like my mother and father knew that they had the gift of music and they shared it with the world as they went about their lives doing what they did, others, got busy with other talents that they recognized early on and went that way. It doesn't mean they didn't have the gift of music, it just meant that that gift was not discovered or as important to them as other talents were.

Okay, so where am I going with this. I came to the realization that not long after discovering that I had these special talents and the gift of music, I began to move quickly forward in my understanding of how chord progressions worked, and it all seemed to happen logically in my head. There is no substitute for practice, but I found that as I was practicing, the tediousness and redundancies did not bother me at all and I found a kind of joy in my eventual progress. I wanted to be a singer/songwriter for a long time, but there was something in my DNA that told me, of course you can do that—you and your ancestral line were instilled with musical talents from our Heavenly Father *many* generations ago with the gift of music, therefore, you born with the gift of music! How cool is that?

Long story short, you, my children and grandchildren also inherited my DNA which means that you too have these special talents and the gift of music. IF YOU WISH, you only need to search for and discover them within, to magnify your powers. I say, if you wish, because not everyone, even those blessed with these talents will feel the need or want to amplify the music powers within. That is your choice to go in that direction or not, but please know this; not everyone has the special talents and the gift of music like you, and unless you hate music and everything about it, which I'm pretty sure is not happening in your DNA, it costs you nothing to explore this world of music.

One more thing; your talent, that music gift we're talking about is powerful and very much like magic. It should not be used inappropriately. You should not use your powers to hurt others or to puff yourself up and be full of yourself, or to gain advantage at someone else's expense, or to hurt someone that is less talented than you. It doesn't mean you can't be competitive at times or that after you've reached a level of proficiency that you can't go out and make money with your talents. There are many good people in this world that use their musical powers to pay their rent and to buy food. That is okay. You need to value your musical powers and know that if you want the powers to stay, if you want your musical talents to grow, you will need to do it in the spirit of kindness and love and you need to be good.

Now, look inside your being and find your powers and magnify your musical talents. They're all there, you just have to find them and use them wisely. Please know that I love you, and wish you happy hunting.

4

❧

Archive Series - Icon

5

❧

01 - LONELY TOO LONG

- 1991

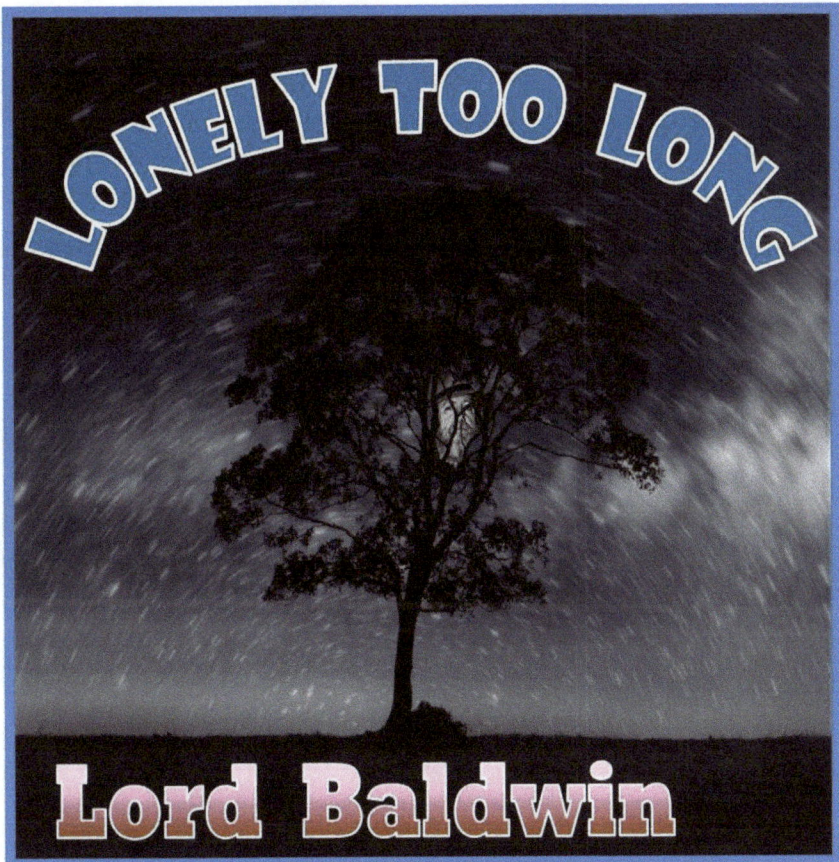

6

NOTES ABOUT THE COVERS:

And so it was, last summer, (Summer 2019), the windows of heaven opened up for "the Unknown Songwriter," and I was suddenly able to get my life's works, all my albums, published. And it got even better when I learned that my albums would then be submitted to all the major streaming outlets, like, Spotify, Amazon Music, iTunes, Apple Music, Pandora, (although at first, Pandora did not make my work available and made me jump through extra hoops to get my material on their site), and other sites in countries I'd never heard of before. I was in a hurry after I had heard of a deadline where submissions would end, (and Spotify did end their, "new Artists" program), but it did not extend to people that had signed up with a distributor.

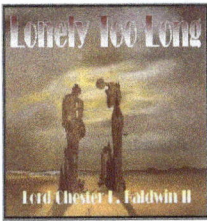

About the Original Cover,...

When putting my album covers together I "borrowed," or to be honest, "Plagiarized" art from Salvador Dali (see below), as well as other famous artists by capturing JPGs from the internet. When I was hurriedly publishing my albums, I found myself in a tight spot when my distributor rejected those covers and I found out that I would need special new art for most of my 44 earlier albums, now known as; "The Archive Series." And so, I started over and created new art for 31 of the 38 covers and did modifications for four of the remaining seven album covers.

About the New Cover,...

I felt that this tree, out in the lonesome evening sky, seemingly abandoned and friendless, certainly all alone, was a good representation for being; **'Lonely Too Long.'**

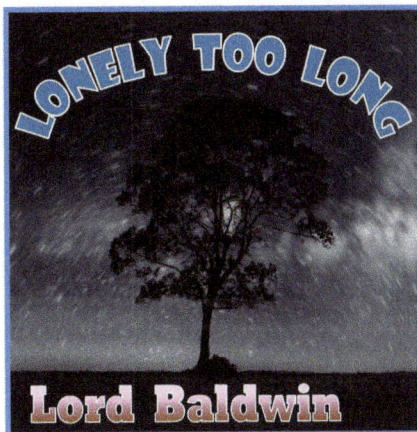

7

LONELY TOO LONG

Lonely Too Long
Right Now, I'm Having A Hard Time
Welcome Home
Relax
I Just Got Paid
Sometime Tomorrow
Times Change
Let It Go
Things Will Get Better,
Somewhere Down The Road
Tomorrow Morning, I Will
Honey, I Got To Go
So Close And Yet So Far
Get On With My Life

8

Lonely Too Long

Well, I'm not stalling around, trying to take up your time.
I'm just waiting around
sighing for you to make up your mind.
I've been living life wrong, all alone and empty without you,
and I've been lonely too long singing this song of the blues.
I'm not breaking my stride till I finally ride on your train.
I won't leave you alone, until you come home again.
Got this feeling so strong,
I'd never known what a woman could put me through.
and I've been lonely too long singing this song of the blues.
Got this feeling so strong,
I've never known what a woman could put me through,
and I've been lonely too long singing this song of the blues.
No, no, no I'm not stalling around trying to take up your time.
I'm just waiting around
sighing for you to make up your mind, please Honey!
And I've been living life wrong, all alone and empty without you,
and I've been lonely too long singing this song of the blues.
Said, "I've been lonely too long singing this song of the blues."

9

Right Now, I'm Having A Hard Time

Maybe tomorrow, I won't be in the wings,
I'll be myself, in the swing of things.
Sometime next week, I won't be carrying this dirt,
and I won't even remember why it was I hurt.
She was the reason I felt good about myself.
Now I here tell she'll be marrying somebody else.
After I've accepted things today, I'll be just fine,
but right now, I'm having a hard time.
Right now, I'm having a hard time.
Can't seem to get myself together anymore,
all my thoughts are scattered as I sit here on the floor.
It's probably too late to figure how I lost the kid,
probably, it's my fault, but I don't know what I did.
She'll be out on her own by tomorrow afternoon,
then she'll take that long drive to her second honeymoon.
Maybe by next weekend, I'll be just fine,
but right now, I'm having a hard time.
Right now, I'm having a hard time.

It wouldn't be so bad, and I wouldn't feel so down,
but in a way, I kind of liked having her around.
I'm still talking to the walls or to some ghost.
This house is kind of empty without her somewhere close.
I've got my future, to live with what's real.
It would be nice if only she could know how I feel.
Maybe next year sometime, I'll be just fine,
but right now, I'm having a hard time.
Right now, I'm having a hard time.

10

Welcome Home

I felt their wrath, though I was miles away.
Before it fell, I then just stayed away.
I had judged their wisdom from my own short years,
I didn't think that they'd understand me down here.
But just the other day, they called me on the phone.
I don't remember what was spoken,
only "welcome home."
Welcome home. Welcome home.
And ain't it funny, the way we all prejudge
our possible future with the one we've grown to love.
Still, I packed my bags and left in my wrinkled suit.
Got on a bus and headed back home, home to my roots.
And just this morning, I stood on that porch alone.
My mother hugged and kissed me
and she cried, "Welcome home, son,
welcome home, welcome home.
All those lectures of repentance never came.
My Father knew my heart and that I had changed.
I can never forget how sympathetic they all cared,
even though I still feel I was wrong to go down there.

The progress of a boy to a man must stand alone.
I have learned from my mistakes,
but I was always welcome home.
Welcome home, welcome home.
Welcome home.

Relax

Relax, take your mind off the tax.
Let the whole mess rot, bring yourself to a stop.
Relax; don't think about that.
Whittle out some wood; do yourself some good.
Cause all this self-destruction you've found,
through your useless running around,
you ought to crash like you can't remember when,
and slow down, just enough so you can think again.
And relax; forget about that fat.
take off your shoes, for goodness sake,
and give yourself a break and relax.
Someday, you won't have to carry that axe,
and you can relax, relax,
you can relax.

12

I Just Got Paid

Throw that casserole in the freezer,
cancel all the plans you've laid.
Come on and put on your favorite dress,
forget about the rest,
we're going out tonight, I just got paid.
It's been so long, since we've had money,
seems like we'll always scrimp and save.
But for now, we're doing fine,
and getting better all the time,
lets' have some fun tonight; I just got paid.
We'll fill up the back trunk with groceries,
pay off the past bills we've made.
Maybe, buy some new shoes,
or we can fix the car's blues,
things are looking up tonight, I just got paid.
We'll get a piece of that American dream,
and not have to hock, borrow or trade.
We ain't riding so high, but we are getting by,
and feeling good tonight; I just got paid, Babe.

13

Sometime Tomorrow

Sometime tomorrow I won't be this tired,
I'll shake out the demons; step out of this feeling of being wired.
Here in my life, I've spent a third of my time in bed,
just searching for a clearing around the bend.
But the work got hard and the work we tried to leave,
seemed to win in the end and here we are my friend to grieve.
I've got to get some sleep before the morning at last.
Work is coming early and fast to my door and I'll be on the floor.
Say goodbye to Betty, hurry up and get ready, fast to work but
steady.
And I know why we've all got to die this way,
with no alternatives, no directions and no dreams.
With nothing but the wars to lose away,
but me, I'm glad for being here to play.
Sometime tomorrow I won't sing this song,
I'll drop this load, head on down the road where I must belong.
Here in my life, I spend two-thirds of my time in doubt,
just searching for that easier way out.
But the work got hard and the work we tried to leave,
seemed to win in the end and here we are my friend to grieve.

Floating to a dream; hope of waking never.
Such a peaceful sleep to last forever,
but a buzzing slowly takes it's toll,
turn off that alarm and try to fill that hole in my head,
as I jump from my bed,
wave to all the family, no time to eat those pancakes, full of rush
but empty.
And I know why we've all got to die this way,
with no alternatives, no directions and no dreams.
With nothing but the bills left to pay,
me, I'm glad for being here today.

I4

Times Change

Times change, people rearrange.
They shift priorities to suit their present needs.
Times change, people get strange.
They trade their past and hopes of tomorrow for today.
We had so much, so close in touch;
a relationship that made us both feel great.
But something changed; became estranged
and now, we never try to communicate.
We had so much together, I thought it would go on forever,
and we knew things would get better in the groove.
I thought our situation, was just a bit strained in relations,
but we were working on preparations to improve.
Hey, but times change, people move out of range.
They shift priorities, that suit their present needs.
Times change over to the strange.
They trade a past and hopes of tomorrow for today.
It wasn't me, but you it seems
needed room to find out all you missed.
On a one-way track, you never did look back
and somehow, I just got crossed off of your list.

We had so much together, so close to our endeavors,
I felt we'd go forever like that day.
You were there to find me, as we traveled down this winding,
I thought you were behind me all the way.
Times change; people rearrange.
They shift priorities to suit the present needs.
Times change; people get strange.
They trade off parts and hopes of tomorrow for today.

15

Let It Go

The evening draws on quickly to the point of no return,
as I carry all this anger beyond the amber's burn.
Thoughts and deep emotions dam up the natural flow,
yet something else inside says that I should let it go.
Questioning and wondering from these feelings I sustain.
Is the need for some small justice
worth the cost of all the pain?
Is it he or she or it that is my vicious foe,
or my stubborn pride that will not let it go.
Dragging around those vague ghosts that pulse within my head,
for some cause, that's long forgotten
and reasons now long dead.
Chasing cold vendettas for some purpose; I don't know.
While all my instincts from inside beg me to let it go.
Somewhere between adolescence and maturity if learned
is wisdom and compassion to temper those feelings burned.
Somewhere between this hurting
and a healing yes, from no
is the warmth of forgiveness if I but let it go.

16

❦

Things Will Get Better, Somewhere Down The Road

"Will I always be this poor?" I heard the young girl say
as she reached into her purse at a grocery store to pay.
"I don't need this, I can do without," I heard her softly speak,
and only filled one bag to hold her for a week.
But things will get better, and we'll be out of debt.
I can feel the good times coming, they just ain't here yet.
It could be a whole lot worse, this ain't a heavy load.
Things will get better, somewhere down the road.
His sign said, "Work For Food; Anything Around".
Sitting on a curb staring at the ground.
"I got a wife and three kids living in a shack,
I just got to bring them food, or else I can't go back."
But things will get better, and we'll be out of debt.
I can feel those good times coming, they just ain't here yet.
It could be a whole lot worse; this ain't a heavy load.
Things will get better, somewhere down the road.
They were living in a van camped out at a park.
He labored all the summer from sun up till dark.

Making just enough to get by; they had nothing left to keep,
still happy every night, he would sing them all to sleep.
Singing, "Things will get better, and we'll be out of debt.
I can feel those good times coming, they just ain't here yet.
It could be a whole lot worse; this ain't a heavy load,
things will get better, somewhere down the road."

17

Tomorrow Morning I Will

Things just get so out of hand when I procrastinate.
Now I'm faced with strong demands and problems that won't wait.
Too many wasted days and nights avoiding all I find.
Too many things swept out of sight and then swept out of mind.
I have put this off so long, I've made a mountain from a hill.
I wouldn't face this yesterday but tomorrow morning, I will.
Some people want to take their time to make sure things are right.
But I'm just scared to face that side and bring things into the light.
Too many excuses not to see her because my time's all gone.
I see now it's much easier to approach this love head-on.
I have put off this so long, it's made a mountain out of a hill.
I couldn't face this yesterday but tomorrow morning, I will.
I thought things were just fine, when I kind of liked it that way.
Now she wants to be mine and is waiting for me to say.
Too many reasons not to love; I over-shadow all the good.
I see now it's a matter of just doing what I should.
I have put this off so long, it's made a mountain out of a hill.
I couldn't face this yesterday but tomorrow morning, I will.
I have put this off so long, it's made a mountain out of a hill.
I couldn't face this yesterday but tomorrow morning, I will.

Tomorrow morning, I will.

18

Honey, I Got To Go

I've done everything within my power
to keep our love from turned sour
yet all in vain, you've got another man.
But let's not just sit and stir the stew,
there's things I'd like to see and do.
I've got to get out there while I still can.
I'm restless like a rolling stone,
and I feel the call of the open road,
that freeway fever's calling me to roll.
Hey Babe, you know I'm not alive,
till I got that Chevy into overdrive
and heading out, Honey, I got to go.

I got to go with the flow of the highways and the roads,
hook my tow rope on some distant southern star.
Got to believe in my dreams as my troubles and my grief's
disappear through the rear view of my car.

I never thought with our first kiss it would finally come to this
I was kind of hoping that our love might grow.

Still things sometimes just don't work out,
and I'm not about to sit here and pout,
I got plans to keep, Honey, I got to go.

I got to go down the road to heaven only knows,
to places I've never seen and never been.
I'm all set, got to get, and for dang sure you can bet
that I won't be coming back round here again.

I'm heading out for parts unknown,
ain't calling anywhere my home.
Like to say where I'll be, but I don't really know.
Maybe some other place and time
but you got your life and I got mine,
I need to run, Honey,... Honey, I got to go.

19

So Close and Yet So Far

So close. So close and yet so far.
So far from where we are.
We are so far from close and then it's time to go.
Good friends; good friends always care.
Always care and share.
Share farewells to friends, as their journey ends.
We knew. Knew then at the start,
someday we would depart
from good friends at heart.
And then, we somehow just lost touch,
with everything too much, in later times we trust.
So close, so close and yet so far.
So far from where we are.
We get so far from close
and want the love to show.

20

Get On With My Life

It's over and done; there's no doubt anymore.
I never caught that hint when she walked out that door.
Trying to put it behind me tears me up deep inside,
but I've got to get going and get on with my life.
I kept thinking that we'd get back together somehow,
but I know her by heart and that'll never happen now.
When I saw her with him, it cut me like a knife,
and I knew time had come to get on with my life.
I held on, hoping we, might share love again,
but its too late to change all of those might have beens.
I thought we had something, but now I just don't know,
while my heart's broken up, says it's time to let go.
Its hopeless to think she'd be back in this home,
but its worse to realize that I'm left all alone.
She has her new world, and I should just cross that line,
to get up, and go out, and get on with my life.

21

MEMOIRS & NOTES - 01 - 'LONELY TOO LONG'

Lonely Too Long

(Written in 1973) - Although it could be argued that "Lonely Too Long" was the first guitar song I ever wrote, it was not. In my pursuit of guitar mastery there were more than a dozen songs prior, but this song is fitting to represent the first song of my first album because this song, which got polished early on and for some time was one of my best live performance numbers, became my signature song. Unlike the Bluesy, "I Been Lonely Too Long" song by the Young Rascals, this song is sung in a "Rock-a-Billy" style that allows me to limber or loosen up while performing it. It's like Campbell's Chicken Noodle Soup that goes down easy and makes me feel good inside.

Side Note:

I arrived back in Portland Oregon in the fall of 1971 and after commuting back and forth with my father from his farm in Aurora 's to Portland every day for a few weeks I landed a job with a Burger Chef restaurant, a block away from the Portland State University. And it was there that I met Diane. She worked the front counter and I worked the back.

Burger Chef Building - Portland Oregon

I may go into more detail about this later, but for now I want to tell this part. People wore uniforms back then, even in burger joints and one afternoon while she was cleaning the milkshake machine, I dropped a handful of ice down the back of Diane's uniform. She jumped to attention and squeaked like a squirrel and then looked back with an, 'I'll-get-back-at-you-for-this' smile. This began our formal acquaintance. We began sitting together, sharing French fries at lunch, and a few weeks later, I had been trying to get up the nerve to ask her if she wanted to go out with me to a movie.

The day I was really ready to ask her, she did not arrive to work. Later, Mr. Ricketts, our manager, told me that she had gone to her home for the holidays and would not be back till after the new year.

It was the first week in 1972 when Diane came back to work and didn't seem to have missed me, but when I saw her, something stirred deep inside and I knew I'd better make a move before someone else sees her specialness and I will remain being a lonely guy.

Diane seemed to bolt when it was time to leave and I found myself having to break away from work. I grabbed my bicycle and quickly headed in the direction I thought I saw her walking down 6th avenue. I saw her from maybe three or four blocks away and she was walking fast. When I finally caught up with her, I positioned myself onto the left side of the bike and kind of jumped down while moving, stepped off, and quick stepped in place, directly behind her.

"Hey." I said, startling her enough to give a quick apprehensive glance behind her. She stopped walking and waited for me to catch up and as we walked together to her apartment, we talked.

After that, I walked with her every night, and when we were both given the opening shift, and started opening the facility in the morning (at 6:00 AM for students to get donuts and coffee), I would meet up with her and I walked her to work every morning.

We went on our first date a week later on a Friday night. The next morning, I went over to see her and pressed the buzzer on the outside intercom to her apartment. "Who is it?" I heard a girl's voice call gruffly back from the intercom speaker. "Diane?" I asked, knowing it was not Diane. "No." she returned coldly. "Is this Diane's apartment?" I asked. "who is this?" the girl replied. "I'm a coworker, and," I began. "She is busy right now." The voice returned and I heard a kind of click that meant the conversation was done.

Eventually I did get invited up to her apartment and found that Diane had two roommates; Elizabeth and Sally and that Sally, (the person on the intercom) did not like me. But Diane did and there were times when I went there, we would go out into the cold deserted stairwell and make out. Sometimes we would be out there for hours.

And so, the girl working the front line along with the guy that worked the back, were no longer, "Lonely Too Long."

Another Side Note:

As a songwriter, we often look to and even have other performing artists in mind to pick up our song to cover it; putting their own special style to it. I had hopes of Elvis Presley doing this number, but alas, four years after its creation, Elvis died of a heart attack, brought on by his addiction to oxycodone barbiturates and so, I marched on.

Yet Another Side Note:

For many years I felt that this song was going to be my ticket to fame and fortune. John Lund, my friend and former Bishop, promised me back in 1975 that he would find a way for the world to hear this song. After he moved away to Utah, I kept thinking he would get in contact with some LDS promoters at BYU or someone in Salt Lake City and I would be on my way.

Time went by, years passed,... it never happened, but I learned years later when I went to Education Week at BYU that my friend John may have gotten busy in life himself,... Dr. Lund had published in two different fields of research,... Dr. Lund's work has taken him on a forty year journey where he has taught as adjunct faculty at major universities throughout Washington, Idaho, California and Utah,... Dr. Lund has lectured in twenty-seven foreign countries in both fields of interpersonal communication and on world religions,... but I feel that he never forgot about Lord Baldwin and he was very happy to see me again years later,... and he sent me a signed book in 2007 that he wrote,

'Mesoamerica and the Book of Mormon: Is This The Place?' And I do wish him well.

Right Now, I'm Having A Hard Time

(Written in 1991) – When I was putting this first album together, this song rose to the top because, at the time, it was one of those songs I was performing locally and was kicking around the block. It felt right to place this song where I did. Songs in the second position on my albums have always been very special and I hold them in high regard. I'll maybe explain this concept in detail sometime later on.

There are a lot of different kinds of love song and I have covered most of them,... like love itself, I write about my reflections and sometimes I have the audacity to offer my unmitigated advice,... then there's loneliness and longing for love, maybe combined with the searching for true love, (or any kind of love), the single and being alone syndrome,... there's that young love and first love contemplations with its complications which could include crushes, infatuations and new loves,... there's the tenderness songs with notes of, 'more than just a friend' closeness affections,... the passion (or hope thereof), and maybe the promise to love,... and then there's desire,... the surrender of self to love,... the dealing with or at least the contemplations of dealing with that restrictive or forbidden love,... there's the compromise,... one of my recurring themes is the regrets of what happened compared to what should have happened,... the cease-fire in hopes of a reunion,... but moreover (and in my opinion), many of the best love songs that try to document the complications and struggles and conflicts of rejections and the break-ups,... and along with the, 'trying to make it all work' to, 'get love back together again,' all the hopes that love with triumph.

Side Note:

I think with this poem, I touched on more than one of the themes or kinds of love songs,... and it is so much easier when you're not just writing from your head but have a real-life model to write from.

My friend Samuel, of whom I was going through Computer Science courses with, was married to Linh, a female who arrived in America in the first wave of refugees from Vietnam and in 1985 she met Samuel in California before they moved here to the Pacific Northwest,... and their relationship after six years was, for whatever reasons, unstable and troubling,... I went to their house for lunch one afternoon during a break in classes,... and I was awestruck with the callous way she treated me, a visiting stranger, and more so, how she insensitively she treated Samuel and even more, how Samuel allowed that venomous relationship to continue without addressing its toxicity. As we were driving back to campus Samuel felt a need to explain and apologize for the way I was treated there in his home. Fast-forward about six months, Samuel told me after class that Linh had cleaned out their bank account and left him. Samuel turned to me and said something to the effect,... "I think I'll be alright tomorrow, or next month, but I'm having a hard time dealing with this, right now." This was a poignant moment that I tried to capture in the words to this poem.

Welcome Home

(Written in 1977 - 1978) - After being baptized in the church I left for New York and fell away from the "Word of Wisdom" and many of the principles I had promised to observe. In my mind there were times that I thought about home on the farm and I could sense the disappointment my dad and his wife Inez were experiencing. And yet, I knew without hesitation, I was welcome to come back home, and one day I did, and I was very well received. This song was a reflection of my apprehensions and joy on coming back home to the farm in Aurora.

In 1990, I had just a handful of songs that I could perform for audiences and this was one of them. As with most of my piano songs, this song was composed and played in the key of "F#" and I did have to strain my voice to get some of it out.

There were many times that when asked to play some piano song, this would be one of the first songs to perform, mainly because the chords were easy and I could remember all the words. There was also a "feel" to the song and it had a good message of hope that I felt was good to place as an atmosphere to set up for the next couple of other piano songs.

Side Note:

I got an audience feel for this song and it's draw or appeal to the younger crowd, after I performed it to a large gathering of over 300 people while on a temple trip to Idaho Falls in 1979. (I was 29 at the time, but I still felt out of sync with kids 12 to 18 years younger).

Aside from the fact that I was nervous and made a few mistakes (the crowd didn't pick up on them anyway), the performance and my song was very well received and as the audience was clapping, albeit, maybe obligatory, the whole experience nonetheless felt celebrated and glorious.

Another Side Note:

Later that year I auditioned for a special musical showcase put on by the Olympia-Lacey LDS Stake Center to showcase the locally talented Mormons, (members of the Church of Jesus Christ of Latter Day Saints). Here was this song about a prodigal son that was welcomed back home by understanding and considerate parents—what an inspiring piece. I prayed for the strength and insight to be with me and for the song to be performed well, so as to touch the judge's heart and be received in the compassionate spirit that I wrote it.

To my delight, in the audition I performed this song almost flawlessly. To my disappointment, the then Stake President, Leslie Gilbert, (of whom, later on, I became very good friends with), said it was not quite what they were looking for. I explained that I had other material, but it was of no use; they did not want me.

I was crushed, feeling that, because the Stake President was in a direct communication with God, it was God himself that had, as a final point, disapproved and rejected me, as well as my wonderful heart-felt song. It would be a long time before I performed for the church again.

Yet Another Side Note: In those days, (and is still today in many ward and stake meetings), the guitar and guitar music was banned from being used in the chapels, even to play spiritual things like, Silent Night.

Relax

(Written in 1972) - With the world going way too fast for me, I just wanted to get off the freeway and slow that Morris Minor down. Eventually I did. In late spring of 1970, when I finally decided to get a guitar, I bought a nice Yamaha 12-string guitar from a small shop in Woodstock, New York. (kind of like the Guild that John Denver is holding in his first album). I knew very little about how to play it and less about how to tune it.

The end of that summer with my friend Harvey and his girlfriend Lisa, I helped finance and copiloted a car trip from New York, through parts of Canada, and then down and across the Midwest area of the United States. I was wrong to think that the fake alligator guitar case would protect that guitar from the intense heat of Nebraska, Iowa, Arizona and Southern California.

By the time I got back in Portland, the taunt strings had warped the neck so badly that afterwards I could only play it as a steel guitar. I was heartbroken and depressed after the guitar shop was less than optimistic about the guitar's repair. For a long while afterwards I was trying to figure out how I might afford to get another guitar.

Side Note: Right after I got set up in an apartment in Portland, someone broke in and stole some of my albums, my 72-reed chromatic harmonica that my mother had given me for my 18th birthday, (and after years of getting a harmonica every year for my birthday, the last harmonica, my mother ever bought me), and of course, the warped Yamaha guitar and hard shell case with its fake alligator skin covering.

It was almost a whole year before I could afford another guitar and I wrote this song on that new guitar; a 1963 Fender, King concert acoustic with an internal bracing system; a 1" diameter rod of aircraft aluminum that runs parallel to the strings from the front to the back of the body, stabilizing the enormous pressure, placed on the top of an acoustic guitar by the string tension to bridge,. of which, my son Stephen still has possession of.

I Just Got Paid

(Written in 1990-91) - I worked at this place called JW Electronics off and on for over 16 years. One day, after a financial crisis unfolded on October 19, 1987, a day known as "Black Monday," when the Dow Jones Industrial Average dropped 22.6 percent,... some bank people from Sea First Bank, a subsidiary of the Bank of America, came into the JW Electronics store and called their loan,... which in fact, caused JW Electronics to go into bankruptcy proceeding,... and after a three-year struggle to turn things around or reinvent themselves, in March of 1990, after being open over 25 years, JW Electronics had to close its doors. A month prior, in February, I found out that Diane was expecting again, (birthday present), and I was one of those workers that lost their job and then ended up on unemployment.

I enrolled in the Spring quarter at South Puget Sound Community

College and worked on a Computer Science degree. In October of that year, my daughter Allison had just been born, making our family with nine kids and two adults now counting to eleven.

We were living on unemployment insurance and church welfare. At that time, church-wise, we were in the Olympia Second Ward, and things were not going well with our food circumstances, partially because our Bishop's Storehouse food order was continually not getting turned in. After having to drive up to the Bishop's Storehouse in Kent every two weeks, and us scraping bottom, hard to find gas money, I reached down into the dregs of my soul and dignity, and applied for food stamps.

Diane was reluctant to get involved, but my situation was dire so I went in alone, repeatedly, did all the paperwork, (and there was a lot of that), sat in the offices being gawked at and seemingly judged by everyone else there. Not cool.

After we started receiving the food stamps, most of the time I had to do the shopping too because Diane hated the way the checkers at the grocery stores judged and treated her. It was humiliating, but I felt it was the best thing to do at the time.

In my last year at South Puget Sound Community College, (SPSCC), I got this temporary job as an internship, working with computers for the Washington State Parks Department. Although the work caused my GPA to take a slight dive, I still remember how good it felt to be working again and earning my own money.

And of course, Diane was so ready for us to stop getting food stamps and taking government assistance.

This poem was written right after I got my first paycheck. There is an intrinsic joy when it comes to getting paid and having money to spend, even if it is for groceries and bills; this song still makes me feel good. And yes, just like in the song, I did fill up the back trunk of my beat up 1967 Chevy Nova with many bags of groceries.

Side Note:

I have written many songs to and for Diane, or with her in mind, and it still surprises me to find which songs she ends up liking or not.

Besides some obvious songs that have some sentimental value for whatever reasons, because this is her most requested song for me to play for her, I feel that she remembers that day when that first new check arrived; it is probably her favorite all-time song.

Sometime Tomorrow

(Written in 1978) - I was driving home from a Portland A&W Rootbeer Stand after polishing off a root beer float when this guy on the car radio said that we would all end up spending a third of our whole life in bed, mostly asleep. So, I wrote this song.

Perhaps the first of many songs that kind of seem to whine about how things could be but due to the "poor boy" syndrome of depraved circumstances, looking towards another time later, (maybe sometime tomorrow), to fulfill my dreams, because it sure wasn't happening then.

Over time the poet in me has come to be thankful for those experiences so as to help me feel the pain and suffering and degradation and loss of dignity so as to appreciate things if and when they did get better. I feel it has helped me to have more compassion and charity in my being and had hopefully made me a gentler, kinder me.

Side Note:

This song still has a certain charm that the Baldwin brothers, (Ray, Richie, myself and sometimes, Charlie) recognized and so, performed, (or jammed in Ray's attic and basement), a lot in the 70s and 80s.

Times Change

(Written in 1990) – I was jamming with my brothers, Richard and Ray one weekend and after some hours of radical jamming, the beginnings of this song came out. On the two-hour trip back to Olympia, I played with the words in my head, and when I got home, I couldn't find any paper to document the words, and so, being in a rush, I wrote the majority of this poem on the back of a phone bill that was sitting on the kitchen table. I think this was the first poem I ever wrote with the aid of a computer, but not even with WordPerfect 4.2, which was the thing at the time, but as a lab tech in the computer resource center, I had access to a computer program called, Pascal, which worked fine as a text file. This poem is about realizing that attitudes and relationships with each other can and will change.

Side Note:

in the last few months before JW Electronics folded, there was only about nine people still working there. Ron, one of the salesmen, bought the remainder of the stock and reopened with another name. He, his wife, Kathy and a few of the other employees stayed there. I was not asked or seriously considered until things took off for them— but by then, I was heavily into my second year of college and I passed. I did not have to wonder why I was not considered; I was not valued. And that whole acceptance and non-acceptance thing is truly what this poem was all about.

Another Side Note:

This was, (and maybe still is) one of Richie's favorite songs, and he requested it all the time, not sure what it was in the music or the words of the poem that touched him but I was always game to jam on the song.

Let It Go

(Written in 1987-88) – In 1988, my dad and Inez, my stepmother, who were married for 28 years, decided to get a divorce. The reasons for the split, both for my dad and Inez, were varied and depended on whom you talked to, but the point was, and looking at it from a later perspective; there was no real strong determinable reason for the separation, it was all because of things; even from years earlier, remembered or not remembered, attitudes, needs not being met, words not being said and situations not being resolved, all culminating to this eventual happening. Like the end results of so many other marriages, much was frivolous, irrelevant and petty. I was torn between blood relations, (my dad), and this woman that I had known as my other mother since 1968.

I made an effort to maintain a personal relationship with Inez, and through many phone calls through the watts line at JW Electronics, I helped her to a degree, to get her disheveled life back together and I helped to resettle her into grandpa Baldwin's old house in upper Milwaukee.

Even as I was helping her to put her life back in order, things were still so strained that she constantly made negative referrals to all of my dad's faults; of which was sometimes, TMI (too much information), and things I didn't need to know. To make matters worse, one day I was literally shut out of her life. I had made prior arrangements to come down to Portland to install an air conditioner, but when I went over to the house, I found that she was not at home. Also, the emergency key was gone and all of my subsequent calls then and afterwards, were left unanswered. I called my sister Kathy, (Inez's baby), but she was clueless.

After a long while I found out that Inez had felt inspired to marry some man that was dying of a number of things and it was later that I found out that my California brother, Jack, (a brother that I had become ostracized from, over ten years earlier), had written a letter to her demanding that she sever her relationship with me. I was enraged. I was mad that Jack, who never called or kept in contact with either Inez, my dad or me, for years, should think he had any business in her or my life. I was also sad that she allowed my brother Jack to control her even after the divorce. But I was also annoyed that I would let my feelings get the best of me and that I would surrender to that anger.

One night I was tinkering on the piano with chords in the key of D and the simple, but emotional music I was playing soon moved me so much so, that I was up until 3 AM writing down the words to the poem and polishing the chord progressions on my mother's piano. The song, about forgiveness and letting the past go to heal one's self inside, moved me, calmed me down and opened my eyes to my own shortcomings.

Side Note:

After my son Christopher passed away in 1992, I saw Inez again when she showed up at the funeral. She didn't know that I knew the truth about the Jack thing and I never brought it up. Eight later, her chronically ill husband had passed away, she had moved to Arizona to live with my sister Wendy, and then moved to St. Lewis to live with my sister Kathy.

In the fall of 2000, she was visiting Portland and got deathly sick. Diane and I went down to visit her and I went a second time when she had a relapse days later. Almost exactly a year later while living in Saint Lewis, she got sick again, this time with a form of leukemia and after a very short battle, she passed away on the 9th of September of 2001. Her remains arrived in Portland the night before the terrorist attack on 9/11.

Another Side Note:

The morning before Inez passed, I called at 6:30 to see how she was doing. In a tired and worn-out voice, she asked me to call her later. When I did call later that Friday afternoon, Inez was unable to talk on the phone.

Years later I wrote a song to document my feelings of sadness and inadequacy to be denied the opportunity to see her before she passed away. I recorded the song, 'I Got The Call Saturday Morning' and that song can be found on the last Archive Series album, (#44) "The Universe Within."

Things Will Get Better, Somewhere Down The Road

(Written in 1991) – This song was a chronicle of short events that happened to me during one summer weekend in 1991. On a Friday afternoon, I was buying hot dogs and marshmallows for a campout at the Top Foods store in Olympia, when a girl in the grocery line looked up at me with a concerned look and said in a sad but hopeful voice, "Will I always be this poor?" She then rummaged through her stuff and prioritized her needs, leaving some of her supplies behind. As I was driving away, I saw a man holding a 'Will Work For Food' sign and I was moved. I sang, "Ain't These Them Hard Times We Been Talking About?" to myself as I drove home.

That night, after getting the family tent set up at the Margaret

McKenney Campgrounds in Capitol Forest, I interacted with a young man who, with his wife and two kids, were living in a run-down camper van. We were all sitting at a campfire; my family and his, when I said, "Things Will Get Better," to all of them. The young man smiled sadly as he nodded his head in acceptance and maybe with a sincere hope for the future, but that look on his face moved me to write the words to this poem, about hope in adversity; knowing that in spite of (or maybe because of) adverse circumstances, we ultimately determine our own attitude and happiness from our faith and hope in ourselves and humanity.

Side Note:

I hoped that the feel of this song and the message of hope might shine through the desperation of the circumstances, and I knew that my hopes were realized after my son Chet would sing along to the song as I played it on the cassette player in my 67 Chevy.

Another Side Note:

This is a bit off track but long before I left JW Electronics, I armed my 67 Chevy Nova with a killer sound system. Collectively, counting all the speakers in the car strategically placed from triads in the back window to box speakers under the dash and tweeters up by the windshield,... oh, and I had a pair of, **MTX TS102**, 10" 2-way truck

box speakers, and all together I had 17 speakers, (I know, odd number but that's how it worked out), pushing out sound by a 200-watt amplifier,...

When it was cranked with *Jimi Hendrix* or *the Beatles* or *Billy Idol* or *Rick Ashley* or *Living Colour*, Chet, Lori, Liz and Meridith were enthralled; it was all glorious.

Yet Another Side Note: That Switchcraft, No. 668, Stereo Selector Switch, with 3 RCA Type Inputs Jacks and

Rotary toggle switch is still serving me well and is still in use as I toggle between the inputs of my **Yamaha PSR 500** keyboard and the **Behringer V-Ampire** head guitar amplifier. Sometimes you really do get what you paid for.

And Yet Another Side Note: Those **MTX TS102**, 10" 2-way truck box speakers, which I got from George Neff after I recorded everything I had of Dylan's onto cassettes for his son,... those speakers were ill-fated, as one evening, Lori and Christy Gardner pulled into Christy Gardner's driveway after midnight to sleep overnight, and this was Lacey Washington where a lot of military families lived,... a sketchy place to live and arguably at the time, the a highest crime area in all of Thurston County,... and Lori had the stereo blasting,... and when Lori woke up the next morning, she found that most of the speakers, my cassette deck, all of my cassettes including many of my own musical creations, as well as an assorted collection of other prized electronic equipment had been stolen.

That is,... well, that is the story I got at the time, but I have, over the years, been given, 'the rest of the story' to other happenings,... like the true story to the smashed back door to the 67 Chevy that was recently confessed,... so I'm waiting for the other shoe to drop on this story,... either way, when that happened, it was long after JW Electronics was gone and there was no way that I could duplicate and revive the stereo again,... but it was so great while it lasted.

Tomorrow Morning, I Will

(Written in 1990) – I had no sooner opened my four-track tape recorder when I got this call from one of the Elders from the church. Someone needed to be moved and my playing with this machine was going to have to wait. I don't remember why it was, but I was wearing a new pair of pants that I accidentally got caught on a screw from this lady's couch and ripped a huge hole in them.

Meanwhile, my annoyance was magnified because the person we were moving out and into a large U-Haul truck was totally unprepared for us to move her. We spent more time boxing and packing her up than loading the truck. I got this tune in my head and I played with some words while I was working there in my holey pants. When I got home, I wrote the words to the poem with the tune in my head and then recorded this song. This is also the first time I played with real sound with sound, so I threw in a few harmonious attempts and then left it the way it was. The feel of the loose recording of this song, (which is about procrastination; not being ready to commit one's self to a relationship in love and life), was almost like not being quite ready in and of itself.

Honey, I Got To Go

(Written in 1991) – I took a trip to Eastern Washington to set up computers for the Parks Dept. and I stayed in a small hotel in Wenatchee. I was watching cable TV, (which I still don't have at home), and I saw a musical video with Johnny Cash in it. I thought, I should write him a song and maybe we could both make some money. I envisioned Johnny's deep voice playing with my lyrics and in a laughing way, say with his Johnny Cash accent, "Honey, I got to go." I have carried feelings of inadequacy of not being good enough. My low self-worth, and even shame interfered with my ability to maintain a good sense of success, including songwriting. I do not think that this recording fully reflected my vision, but I sent the recording and a lead sheet out to the address that I had at the time. My letter and cassette tape came back a month later—"Return to Sender."

So Close And Yet So Far

(Written in 1990) – I had a lot of good friends when I lived in Portland, Oregon, but it seemed like when I moved up here, my ties and relationships with most of them pretty much fizzled out. I was lamenting that passing or rite of passage when this song was written.

Side Note:

Years after we moved to Olympia, I went down to Portland to look up some of my old buddies and maybe rekindle some varied friendships. I managed to spend some time with my brother Richie, but I never found my friend Louie. Although my friend June never moved, I never connected with her either. And it was only after I returned three different times before I made contact with my friend, Mike. We were close most of the time, and yet sometimes it seems we were just so far away from each other. Mike was indifferent and cold on the first part of our reunion and seemed less than enthusiastic to rekindle any relationship. I sat there in a chair facing him, trying to find some commonality and reference point to jump back in to where we had left off. That commonality and reference point never happened because he didn't want it to happen. His curt answers and short attention span to the conversation quickly came to an end as he announced he needed to go sailing the next day. I don't know if it was something that I had done years earlier when we were mountain climbing, or because I was now 17 years older than we had last interacted, or maybe it was because I was 45 pounds heavier, or maybe it was because I didn't smoke pot anymore. Whatever it was, I was no longer his close friend, but just some passing acquaintance that he couldn't wait to have leave his home. With sadness in my heart, I drove out of Mike's neighborhood, headed north onto the I-5 freeway, never to return there again.

Get On With My Life

(Written in 1987-88) – As noted before, it was around this time that my father and his wife Inez got divorced. There were a lot of problems from both sides and the break up galvanized all of us singularly and together. I was on the phone with my dad, listening to his farm problems and church worries; his concerns to other family relationships, and, I listened to his broken heart. I sat there with the phone arched between my ear and shoulder, writing down the words he was saying while trying really hard to continue to be sincere and caring to what was being said. There are many lines in this song that are direct quotes from things he said that night. Just before he hung up, his last heartbreaking words were, "I need to get up and go out and get on with my life."

22

02 - A WORKING
MAN - 1991

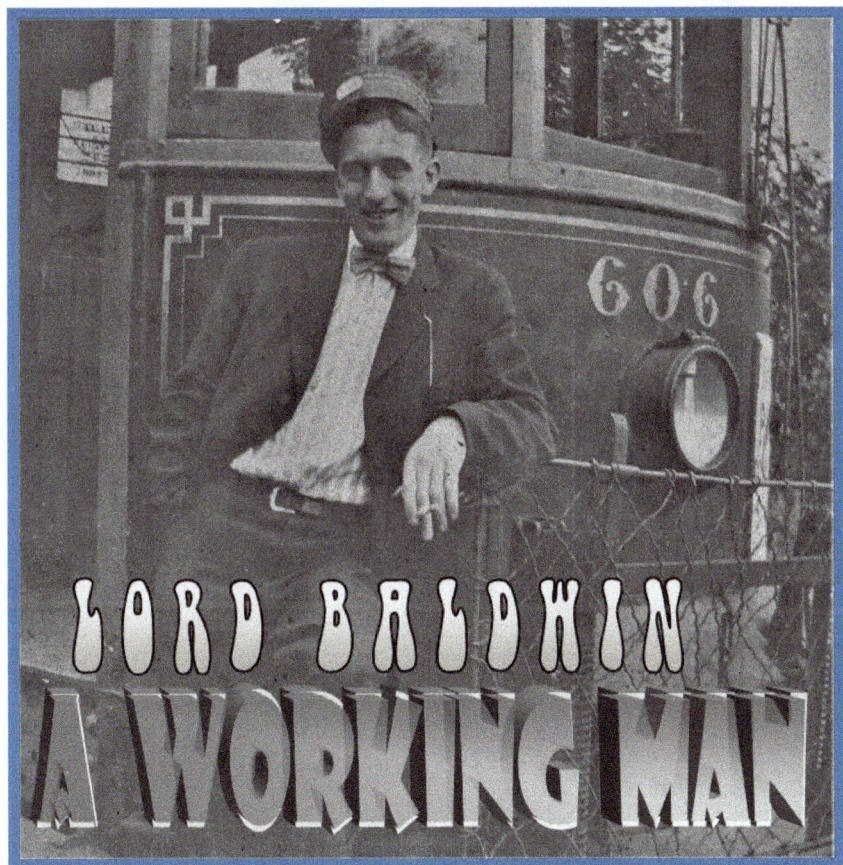

23

NOTES ABOUT THE COVERS:

This new front cover is taken from a picture of my grandfather, **Edward Baldwin,** He worked many jobs in his lifetime, but the one he was most proud of and was working for the Portland Railway Light and Power Company as a Trolley Car Operator and was in charge of the 606 Cable Car; a 3'-6" narrow gauge mountain-climbing electric streetcar, that, like the 506, went up a steep 12 percent grade to the top of Council Crest.

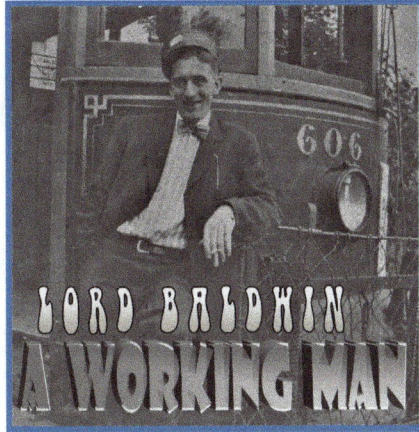

Seen there is my Grandpa Baldwin standing proudly next to his trolley car, the 606, a cable car that he commanded much of his career. If I'm not mistaken, the 606 was the very monumental Cable Car that used to be on display up in Portland Heights up on Council Crest by Healy Heights Botanical gardens.

Although I did not grow up knowing this man or even anything about him but I still felt like this was a good representation of "A Working Man;" a man that was honored and delighted with the work he was doing in his community for and in behalf of the city of Portland Oregon.

Below are the original covers; "Spider Of The Evening" a 1940 painting by Salvador Dali and a quick creation of my own from "borrowed JPGs off the internet in 2001.

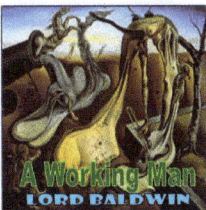

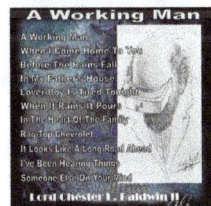

24

A WORKING MAN

A Working Man
When I Come Home To You
Before The Rains Fall
In My Father's House
Lover Boy Is Tired Tonight
When It Rains, It Pours
In The Heart Of The Family
Rag-Top Chevrolet
It Looks Like A Long Road Ahead
I've Been Hearing Things
Someone Else On Your Mind

25

A Working Man

I start my day early, alight breakfast at dawn,
I crank up my truck and in a rush I'm gone.
Work's cut out for me; lots of plans are set,
and what the foreman wants is what the foreman gets.
For a person off the street this job is kind a tough,
but I ain't complaining, I get paid well enough.
Still, there are times I wish I hadn't gone this way,
and maybe used my head and not my back for my pay.
I'm a working man, in a working class.
I get up early and I step on the gas.
I work real hard, do the best I can,
and people know me to be a working man.
I was foolish when young, didn't want to waste time,
I let fast money sway my judgment of life.
So, I came to construction, left my school life behind,
but now I'm stuck in the same old grind.
I got a family to support; obligations to meet,
so I'll be out there in that hot summer heat.
Work gets hard and it hurts now and then,
but I'm working twice as hard to keep up with the younger men.

I'm a working man, in a working class.
I get up early and I step on the gas.
I work real hard; I do the best I can, and people know me,
people judge me to be a working man.
Building houses and apartments to the sky,
in a way it's the same, I'm gonna work until I die.
And what future is ahead with nothing saved from behind?
And if I bust my back I'll only end up on L & I.
Or get laid off every time the industry falls
and live on unemployment till the Boss man calls.
I'm a working man, in a working class;
I get up early and I step on the gas.
I work real hard, I do the best I can, and people see me,
people know me; people judge me to be a working man.

26

When I Come Home To You

Spending too much time each day,
keeping the balance set.
Working my hours away until there's nothing left
when I come home to you.
And Honey, it seems so long,
that we could share our love
and yet, it's not really gone, just waiting to be woke up
when I come home to you.
And Honey, you've grown more precious and lovely each day,
while I let the tasks of the world get in my way.
Although we get by most times with just a kiss and a smile;
Darling, it's you that makes all I do, worthwhile.
It's hard to accept the rest,
when you wonder why and doubt.
The house is in such a mess and the kids got you all burned out
when I come home to you.
And when you can't see those little signs
that show you how much I care
still know that my love and time is waiting for you to share
when I come home to you.

And Honey, you've grown more precious and lovely each day,
while I let the tasks of the world get in my way.
Although we get by most times with just a kiss and a smile;
Darling, it's you that makes all I do,...
it's you that makes all I do, worthwhile.

27

Before The Rains Fall

The words are hard to speak from one like me,
Doesn't matter what happens, only try your best to see,
it's my blood flowing out there along those iron rails.
I'm in search of adventure that can't be found up here
in another place.
Still, you think that I might like to change my ways,
live like you, do the things that your friends and family do.
But I just wouldn't fit in society's mall,
and I can't leave here before the rains fall.
It was easy as a child with no ties to hold me down,
to adapt to the hobo camps hidden outside of town.
Learning how to ride the boxes, and stay clear of the bulls,
how to jump clear of the yard hands as the engineer pulls
in another place.
And you think that I might like to live like you,
just reform from my past and follow what you do,
but I just can't be chained to come when ever you call,
and I can't leave here before the rains fall.
There is so much to be seen and so little time to lose.
If I stop for just one week, all my muscles start to bruise.

Though I feel so strong to stay as your eyes tell me you care,
I must still know in the truth, that my heart is still down there
in another place.
And I don't think I could ever change my ways,
It's not good for me, much more less no good for you.
Though this love is strong I don't fit behind your walls,
and I can't leave here before the rains fall.
And I don't think it would work any other way,
so goodbye my last hope; I might come around some day.
Just to see all your children and know it might have been
someone else as their father and someone else as your friend.
Now the sun rises quickly, I must run with the whistle call,
and I can't leave here before the rains fall.

28

In My Father's House

My father was an actor, he performed upon the stage,
many felt with his great talents he should sure go all the way.
But though he loved the stage so dear he felt his family most,
and he left those dreams he nurtured to follow other roads.
He was driving trucks delivering, cutting most ambitions short
for the values he held highest; a wife and children to support.
And though at nights I'd wonder when I'd see him broke and spent,
were we really worth the sacrifice for all it must have meant?
But in my father's house, we grew up close in touch,
although he worked us hard it was so we could learn twice as much.
Though we never got rich, we all had enough to spare:
lots of trust and understanding, lots of dreams and love to share.
My father was a musician, with nimble fingers he could play,
Singing songs to grace the music. Most thought he was on his way.
But the hours and the money would only sport a single man,
so he left the crowd applauding for a different working plan.
My mother stood beside him, always building him up more,
for she knew the pain he carried and felt the loss he bore.
And for all the disappointment, all was hidden how it feels,
for they loved their family more than themselves or false ideals.

But in my father's house, we grew up close in touch,
although he worked us hard it was so we could learn twice as much.
Though we never got rich, we all had enough to spare:
lots of trust and understanding, lots of dreams and love to share.
With time, his children left his home like brilliant flags unfurled.
All gifted with a part of him to share amongst the world.
His body aged with passing time, waxing over hopes and trust
though he never did regret that he did it all for us.
My father was an actor, he performed upon the stage,
many felt with his great talent he should sure go all the way.
Still at times his distant eyes hints of a dream suppressed,
for a moment he'll be far away, then he'll let it fall to rest.
But in my father's house, we grew up close in touch,
although he worked us hard it was so we could learn twice as much.
Though we never got rich, we all had enough to spare:
lots of trust and understanding, lots of dreams and love to share.

29

Lover Boy Is Tired Tonight

Today has run its course with its turmoil and remorse,
and hassles at work like a man sent to the front.
It's a battle I never win, and I come home all caved in.
A good meal and some sleep is all I want.
So, if you're thinking of me as an opportunity
just because I've turned out the lights,
I'm sorry to say, it'll have to be another day,
because Lover boy is tired tonight.
I've been hard at it all day, with the bossman on my case,
thinking anywhere else is where I ought to be.
When I'm feeling like this, even hunger doesn't exist.
I might fall asleep watching TV.
So, if you've made some plans to attack your man,
after the kids have disappeared out of sight,
better suppress them for now, postpone them for now,
because Lover boy is tired tonight.
It's not anything of you, just something I'm going through,
so drop your guard and know that I still care.
But my ship came in and it sank, I'm riding on empty tank,
and coming into home for repairs.

So, if your love lights' on and you see mine is gone,
don't be upset, I'm sure there'll be other times,
maybe tomorrow, let's say, but for now, there's no way,
because Lover boy is tired tonight.

30

When It Rains, It Pours

Don't look for reasons that might make sense,
there's no logic in what we do.
I know that you've told me, but I'm still kind of dense,
and I just don't understand you.
You feel uneasy, but you don't know why.
you think you need to go home by train.
So I'm on this platform, waving goodbye,
and now it's going to rain.
When it rains, it pours in buckets on me.
It's all at once, no breaks in between.
Everything falls apart at the same time it seems.
When it rains, it pours, and it's always on me.
It doesn't make sense that you'd need to leave,
but if you feel it's right, you've got to go.
I don't understand it, but you know, I believe
when you're ready, you'll head back home.
In marriage, there's so much confusion and doubt,
all the adjustments can be such a strain.
So I'm walking home, trying to sort this all out,
and now, now it's going to rain.

When it rains, it pours in buckets on me.
It's all at once, no breaks in between.
Everything falls apart, at the same time it seems.
When it rains, it pours, and it's always on me.

31

In The Heart Of The Family

You might fail in the task,
be defeated in every turn of the wheel.
You might feel like life isn't worth the hurt
and the sorrow you feel.
You might say and do the wrong things,
be rejected by all of your friends.
You could lose everything that you worked for in life
and have to start over again.
But you can't lose the love, that will always, forever be.
You've a place to always reside, in the heart of the family.
There are times when nothing is right.
There are days when everything is wrong.
In anger and shame, you hang down your head
and its hard to keep going on.
There are times that you might feel lost;
wonder why you're here on this earth.
All the mysteries seem to mock your search for meaning
and you lose your sense of worth.
But you can't lose the love, that will always, forever be.
You've a place to always reside, in the heart of the family.

32

Rag-Top Chevrolet

He's not much into possessions,
out of step and out of touch.
Lifestyles of the rich and famous
don't impress him much.
He has sufficient for his needs, good tires on the rim.
His only passion is the road moving quickly under him.
He held onto the American Dream,
but it somehow slipped away.
He searches for the lost remains
in his rag-top Chevrolet.
Timeless lines of steel and chrome
with an S.S. three ninety-six host.
The smell of the clutch as gear shift down,
winding up the Oregon coast.
He hopes for a good tomorrow,
It's where you're going, not where you've been.
A tank of gas and a bite to eat
and he's on the road again.
He's living what someone else might dream,
doing it all today.

His life is seen through the windshield
of his rag-top Chevrolet.
Like a California evening, the streets all come alive.
Cruising down a byway holding at sixty-five.
Top down, flaps up music cranked,
ain't nothing he's going to miss.
Wind racing through his mind,
doesn't get any better than this.
He hits Mach One with no effect,
shifting gears like child's play.
And he's gliding down the highway
in his rag-top Chevrolet.

33

It Looks Like A Long Road Ahead

When I was young, I thought by thirty-three,
I'd retire, kick back and live at ease.
I passed that goal some years ago working hard instead
and it looks like a long road ahead.

In my running years I figured out,
that with a wife and kids I'd settle down.
Now I can hardly keep them sheltered, clothed and fed,
and it looks like a long road ahead.

A long row to hoe, a long way to go,
with no rest for the weary or the tired.
Working hard to get so far behind in the red,
and it looks like a long road ahead.

I wrote these songs and polished them like pearls,
for the time I'd sing them to the world.
Still, no matter how many songs I write

there is so much left to be said,
and it looks like a long road ahead.

I thought when I labored hard and I did my best,
I'd advance this latter to success.
But I ain't going nowhere fast for this model life I've led
and it looks like a long road ahead,

A long row to hoe, a long way to go,
with no rest for the weary or the tired.
Working hard to get so far behind instead,
and it looks like a long road ahead.
Yes, it does; it looks like it's a long road ahead.

34

I've Been Hearing Things

Word is going round;
hings are not so sound as they seem.
They say, there's no doubt,
and you're running out on me.
I play along like they're all wrong
and we still have the love shining through,
and the words have wings,
I been hearing things about you.

I have tried to ignore
and not hear anymore of all the dirt.
Wouldn't have these doubts
if I thought they we're out
just to make me hurt.
Maybe I'm all wrong because I play along
but you're one I'd never want to lose.
Parties and overnight flings,
yeah, I been hearing things about you.

You play around,

and you'll sure let down your best friend.
They say, what goes around
comes back around in the end.
I hope and pray things are not that way
and the gossip just isn't true,
but this feeling clings,
and I been hearing things about you.

35

Someone Else On Your Mind

Out on the town, dinner and a show,
a good evening out for all I know.
Having so much fun, we hardly notice the time.
Finally, alone,... soft music and lights,
quiet and close, but I'm confused by your eyes,
am I chasing shadows
or is someone else on your mind?

Someone else you see and you touch.
Someone else that loves you as much.
Someone else there in your life,
someone else on your mind.

It's been a long day and you on demand
thoughts carry you away from the moment at hand.
Distractions from love can be many and easy to find.
It's not hesitation, or you trying to stall,
but it's like your heart isn't in this at all,
like you're far away,
with someone else on your mind.

Someone else you see when I'm gone,
someone else that you depend on.
Someone else there in your life,
someone else on your mind.

Alone in the night, looking at stars,
thinking of all we had that was ours.
A good home, family, friends, all thoughtful and kind.
Have I been fooling myself, not seeing the light,
Was it something I did, or didn't do right?
Am I imagining things,
or is someone else on your mind?

36

MEMOIRS & NOTES - 02 - 'A WORKING MAN'

A Working Man

(Written in 1985) – In 1972, I was working at Burger Chef as a night manager during the evening and I worked in construction building a concrete bridge during the day. To complicate things, I had no car and rode my bike about 15 miles to and from work every day. This did not last of course, and I was asked to choose one or the other.

With a promise of more money, a better managerial position and better hours I chose the Burger Chef restaurant. Within six months I was let go. The new general manager that moved down from one of the Seattle Burger Chef restaurants was an older woman that only wanted young girls working for her, (seriously) and I was let go and put out on the street. I went back to the construction site where I was told, "No. you made your choice." It was then that I realized that except for certain cases, if you quit a job that needed you, you will probably never get rehired there.

Side Note:

In the late seventies and early eighties, I was an unhappy person going nowhere, in my or in my music. With things stagnant in career at

JW Electronics, my perspectives narrowed and it became evident that my songwriting was in a tailspin with everything else.

Another Side Note:

After being fired from JW Electronics, (by my brother-in-law) in 1982, and after a series of different short-term jobs, I went to work at the Forest Funeral Home and Cemetery in Olympia. It was there that I regained a positive perspective on life again. It was there that I started feeling good about myself and my direction in life. It was there that I started to write positive, significant songs again. This song, which is a culmination of experiences in my life is one of those.

When I Come Home To You

(Written in 1983) – Diane was at a special luncheon at Relief Society Thursday afternoon on June 2, 1983. This just happened to be our tenth wedding anniversary, so, knowing this occasion was happening, I drove to the church in the 1972 Mercury Marquis station wagon that had been converted into a hearse, walked in carrying my guitar and a bunch of yellow carnations, (from the funeral home), and without a word, I handed the flowers to Diane, who was three months pregnant with Stephen,... and I got up on the stage, briefly explained that it was our **tenth anniversary**,... I sang this song that I had written the night before about how we get so preoccupied with the workings and demands of life that we forget to share our burdens and problems with that person we love. This was an awakening to that truth. And, then with a smile, I abruptly left. This of course surprised Diane and all the other ladies there, but the funny thing is, years later, Diane didn't remember much about the happening, just that it did happen. I remember because I had to leave to get back to the funeral home because there was a body there that needed embalming.

Side Note:

Over the years, this song has followed our lives as a reminder of how things don't always go the way we envision them to go, as parents and best friends,... things happen,... kids are relatively unpredictable especially after they turn into teenagers,... we now try not to get too preoccupied with the workings and demands of life,... and we continue to share our burdens and problems with that special person we love.

Before The Rains Fall

(Written in 1969) – In 1966 my Grandpa Scarbrough (my mother's father) fell sick and mother and I moved him into the big yellow house in the Westmoreland section of Portland that we were living in. Because he was bedridden, he got his own room downstairs next to the kitchen (and a bathroom), and while mother was at work or away, it became my sole responsibility to take care of him when I got home from school.

He wasn't too difficult to take care of, at least, after a while, but he just seemed to want someone to talk to and someone listen to him and his stories. From those many times I sat with him I learned a great deal about him; more that even Mother ever knew.

Many of his stories were so vivid that I wrote songs and stories about them. His life experiences were rich and compelling, and I envisioned myself as the protagonist. Much of his life has become a part of me, remaining with me to this day.

The lyrics to this song illustrate only one of the many parts of his past and his life, being a cowboy, chasing rainbows, riding the rails as a hobo, living the life of the wanderer before he finally settled down and creating roads driving a lot of different construction machinery, especially a road grader.

Side Note:

When Grandpa Scarbrough passed away, my mother, my brothers Richie and Charlie as well as my sister Mary were living in Browns Mills New Jersey. I was a senior in Pemberton Township High School. Mother suggested that, because I had been taking care of him in 1966, that I should go back to Portland with her to the funeral. Because Richie and I were working every weekend upstate New York in the Catskills at the Concord Hotel I needed to call Chick to ask him to give us some time off, which he did. So, we flew to Portland. Mother ended up taking everyone, but I appreciated the nod of thanks from her. (for more on this part of the story, see Side Note to, "In My Father's House").

Another Side Note:

The words to this song fell out one afternoon while I was up in the hayloft at my dad's farm, not long after Grandpa Scarbrough passed away. The music followed later and the whole thing was put together sometime thereafter.

In My Father's House

(Written in 1978) – I came to downtown Portland to watch my father in a theatre production called "George M" In 1978. It was about the life and works of George M. Cohen. Seeing my father up there on the stage with a leading role (Sam H. Harris, George's partner), I was greatly impressed. His acting was flawless and his singing was outstanding. I went back to the farm that night and talked with him at great length. I found out many things that I never knew or took for granted. And although my relationship with my father did not begin until I was 18 and a senior in high school, I began to see and know another side of the man that is my father.

For most people, self-centeredness prevents an understanding of their parents and their parent's motivations, dreams and aspirations, but it was wonderful, even though it was years later, to really know something of the woman who is my mother or the man who is my father. This song was, from my perspective, an accurate representation of how things were.

Side Note:

When I arrived on the farm in December of 1968 with my brother Richard, we were taken in and made part of the family. My dad was happy to delegate all the farm chores to the two incoming young men who, were happy to discover the life on the farm and the strength of a semi-stable household.

Another Side Note:

Although my brother Ray reported that he felt the song was a warped view of things, I grew up without a good father image and Ray had never lived in fear of cruelty and ill-treatment from an alcoholic, abusive man that cared nothing for how I felt. I can say that, for me, this song correctly portrayed my father's values and dreams and even the way things were. I let Ray know that as far as I was concerned, the house that he grew up in and the one I experienced when I was there, were two different environments.

I can tell you what it's like NOT to have a father when I grew up,... instead, I had to live with a stepfather named Senior for twelve years,... and I'd like to say I was brave,... but I was not,... I lived in fear and anxiety for most of my life,... fear and loathing for the man who would be me surrogate father,... instead I was with my mother's husband who was a man that did not want to be my father or to be a part of my life,... when Richie and I got to live with my father in 1969,... we found a loving, caring individual that was genuinely happy within his life doing, not everything, but doing a lot of things he wanted to do,... he was in a lot of front-stage plays in Portland,... with more than walk-on parts too,... and he could sing,... my father had a Broadway carefree approach to singing his songs and my father was a musician and he had played in an accordion band when he was twelve,... and I loved it when he played a polka tune,... and I guess it was probably him that influenced me in so many ways,... and there weren't enough time where he and I would jam in his living room,... good times,...

Yet Another Side Note:

After we attended Grandpa Scarbrough's services, my mother asked if we wanted to stop to see our father on his farm in Aurora Oregon. Richie and I thought it might be cool to see what he looked like and to see our older brother Ray,... Rusty. What we did not know was that, after my bout in California (being in the LA Juvenile Hall for most of a month), my mother was worried about us. It was a different world back then and a lot of kids were going to juvie or jail if the authorities were mean-spirited, and in New Jersey, especially around Fort Dix, they were. Another factor to this story was that our country was still in middle of the Vietnam era where most of the authorities felt that the younger generation was against the war, (which was pretty accurate), so they seemed to hate all teenagers. The short version of this story was that we thought we were visiting my father, but in reality, we got dumped off at my dad's place on the farm and my mother flew back to New Jersey the next day.

Lover Boy Is Tired Tonight

(Written in 1979) – There was a time when electronic parts and end products were flying out the door at JW Electronics, that I was allowed to work a lot of overtime. . By the time I wrote this song, Lori was going on 6, Chet was 3, Liz was almost 2 and Meridith had just been born. There I was working all day picking orders and then well into the evening either stocking shelves or picking more orders. If I was industrious enough, I would make an extra three to five hundred dollars a month. This extra money was great for paying our bills and getting by, but unfortunately it played havoc with my family life. From Monday through Thursday, I was hardly ever home. This song reflected my frustration with trying to keep everything going only to come home and be an inadequate father and moreover, husband. This opportunity of working overtime passed after the next year and we went back to being a happy, but dirt-floor poor family.

When It Rains, It Pours

(Written in 1991) – Richie came up to Olympia, (only three times in 28 years, but I've only been down there four times, so we're even),... and we were jamming when we came up with this tune. After the poetry was written and the music recorded,... I went down to Portland to share the finished project with him, but he was adamant that it needed to be "It never rains but pours." Still, the song was already written and recorded and so, remains what it is today. Richie used to like to pull this one out and sing it wrong just to bug me,... and it did.

In The Heart Of The Family

(Written in 1991) – In 1991 I was working an apprenticeship at the Washington State Parks Department. This was almost like a dream come true, with real benefits and a salary that was a lot more than I was making when I left JW Electronics.

But suddenly I was exposed to an office that had hundreds of single working women, some mothers, some not, some bitter about their circumstances and most that were not happily married were disillusioned and unhappy with the way things were in their lives. I wrote this song with them in mind, thinking that their unhappiness and unresolved feelings could possibly be redeemed just by restoring ties with their immediate families.

This song was a shout out to people that needed not to give up on life and instead to say, that that one thing that might be missing from their life could still be there within their home,... From the philosophy that man is inherently good and has this light of Christ in him or her,... no matter how far they stray or get away from what their strained ties to their past might be,... they probably have someone; a parent, a brother or sister, a cousin or grandparent or just someone somewhere that has become a close part of them and their life,... someone that still loves them, and that love is reason enough not to give up or give into despair. This was ideologically based, of course, but no more than the Beatles singing, *"All You Need Is Love."*

Rag-Top Chevrolet

(Written in 1988) – This song personifies a possible way of life for a person unbound by responsibilities and ties to others, motivated by the need to move forward and see the world but with a free American spirit blowing through his or her hair. One summer evening, on my way home from work, there is a small convenience store/gas station that I frequent at times, especially when I don't want to drive all the way into town. One Saturday morning I had stopped to get gas when a

1966 Chevy Chevelle pulled up to the pumps next to me. It was painted Artesian Turquoise and that paint job had at least three coats of clear, that, even on that overcast day made the car sparkle and look like it had just rolled off the assembly line. I have always wanted a convertible, and moreover a 50's or 60's Chevrolet convertible, but this Chevelle was awesome. As the driver was pumping the gas, he opened the hood to check the oil and noticing I was admiring his car from a distance, he waved to me and asked if I wanted to see the powerhouse. I replied that I did and came over to his car. The driver then pointed to the engine and said, "That's a high performance 396 cubic inch, 6.5-liter engine." Seeing that I was impressed, he smiled and said, "yeah, it flies, man,... really flies." He told me that he was on a road trip to see the west coast but that he had a friend in the area that he came to see and now he was getting a tank of gas and a bite to eat before continuing on his way to the Washington coast line to drive the scenic route through Oregon and California to end up in San Diego. I thought how neat it would be to have that experience in my 67 Chevy Nova with a muscle engine, a rag top and an endless road. And thus, the song was created.

It Looks Like A Long Road Ahead

(Written in 1984) – Memorial Day at a cemetery is the busiest day of the year. People that never come to visit all year long come on that day. On Memorial Day, 1984, as the cemetery Sexton, I was out, running around the cemetery grounds helping those people find their dead relatives plots or spaces when this song came to me. I thought, "When I was young, I thought I'd be retired by now," and, "I've passed that goal some years ago, and it looks like it's still gonna be a long road ahead." We all have dreams and plans and ideas about how things can, should or might possibly someday be, but there might also be a realization that that dream has stumbled and yet, life goes on anyway, with or without me participating. Anyway, a tune came into my head and as I ran back and forth from the grounds to the office building, I would stop and write more to this song. By the end of the day, I pulled out the old, brat up guitar I had stashed in the Cherry Wood casket. And without needing any chord manipulation or alteration, I finished the composition.

Side Note:

This song turned out to be my father's favorite. It is the song he asks me to sing when I am down at the farm in Aurora Oregon with my guitar. He wanted me to find Roger Miller and have him sing it for me. "Make you a ton a money." My dad said. I could not make the connections and Roger died six years later.

I've Been Hearing Things

(Written in 1992) – I was at a school carnival when a friend came up and started talking to me. He said, "I been hearing things about you" in a joking manner, but I wasn't reading the joke and looked at him seriously. He then said "Hey, I'm joking." I realized the power of the moment and wrote down the phrase on a cardboard sleeve of a junk carnival prize. I got home that Saturday night, waited till everyone went to bed, wrote the words, figured out the chords and recorded the song. In writing this song I envisioned some of my experiences in junior high where I would be in the cafeteria or walking out of a class when someone, usually a concerned fried, would tell me something about a girl I was, "seeing" and then I'd have to confront the girl to see what was true. Unfortunately, I can't remember a single time when the gossip was not true; such was the unfortunate state of affairs I dealt with in Jr. high, but there was a lot of material of betrayal and secrets to work with. So, I went to bed after 2:30 AM feeling great because I thought the song was a hit, but the next day, after playing it for Diane, I became indifferent to it. Then, after I had cautiously performed the song in public, I knew it was as good as I had originally thought it was.

Side Note:

As you may find reading entries in the future albums, Diane has not always been a good gauge for my ongoing work. I can say that when she likes a song, that song usually has something, but if she doesn't like it, it may need some tweaking, but it may still have something, but is just not appealing to her.

Someone Else On Your Mind

(Written in 1991) – At the Parks Department I was talking to a young woman while fixing her computer and we got to talking about things at home. She said that for the past few days her husband had been rather distant and detached. She said that she felt it was because of his new job and how much overtime he had to put in and she was patient for him to stabilize any day now.

A couple of weeks later she told me they were separated because she found out he was fooling around with someone at that new place he was working at. I thought about how certain signs had been evident even from the start and approached writing the song from that stand-point. After working for a while at the Parks Department, I discovered WordPerfect 5.1 for DOS and how easy it was to write and edit the words for songs, (lyrics). With many good musician friends in the Second Ward jamming with and cheering me on, I was invigorated and inspired to write more songs, especially in the Country & Western format which was cutting edge at the time. So every day from noon till one I would sit at my station, eat my lunch and work on songs. This was one of them.

Side Note:

This song deals with the suspicious nature of the brain and the tricks that the mind can play on you once you've embraced the thought or the possibility, regardless if it's true or false. It was brought to my attention that maybe I was too preoccupied with this cheating thing, seeing as how three out of eleven songs dealt with the subject, but I don't think so, it was just a coincidence.

37

❦

03 - FOREVER FRIENDS

- 1992

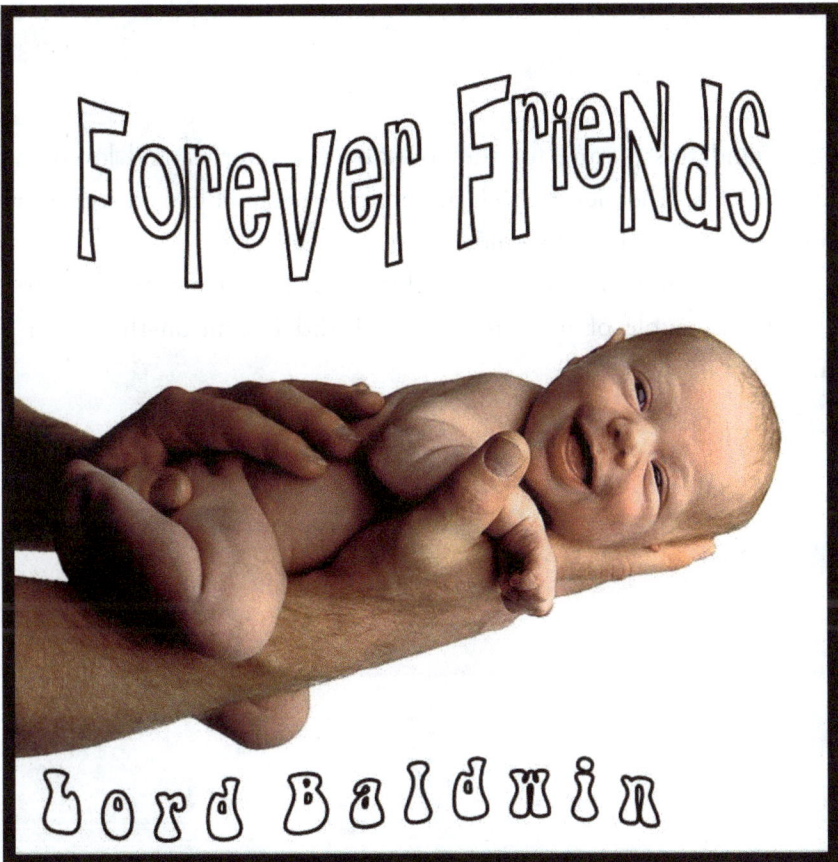

38

NOTES ABOUT THE COVERS:

I found this picture for the cover on the internet and loved the concept. Also, the picture itself did not get rejected by my distributor/publisher so I thought it would be okay.

Our daughter Allison was, at this time, just celebrated her first birthday a couple of months prior and, did I mention that I am a family man?

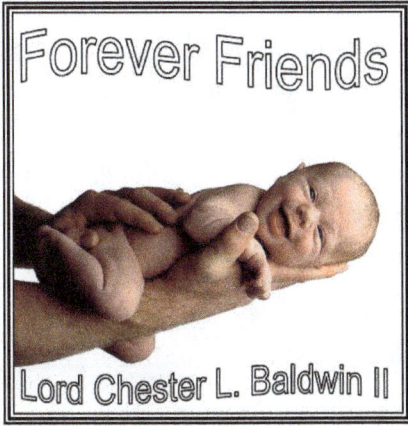

Original Front Cover - 03

When we had our first child, Loren (Lori) in 1973 we went to Lamaze classes at, the Good Samaritan Hospital in Portland, (ironically, the same hospital I was born in). With a goal to build a mother's confidence in her ability to give birth, the Lamaze technique offered information on prepared childbirth techniques, and through the presentation of classes that could help pregnant women understand on how to cope with the pain in ways that both facilitated labor and promoted comfort, including relaxation techniques, movement and massage.

In one of those classes (that we took together), one of the presentation instructors commented that when a baby is newly born, their hearing, their sight, as well as most of their other senses would not be fully developed until the child was two or three months old. That meant that the child would not be able to recognize us for four or five weeks. And if they smile it's only because the baby has gas.

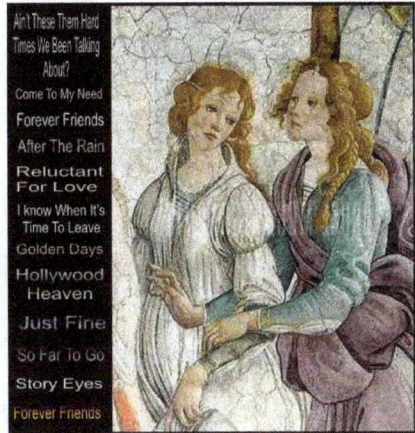

Original Back Cover - 03

As a father of ten children, I can tell you that that person was wrong. Hours after Loren (Lori) was born, I mean hours, Lori could not only see me, but could track my movements as I moved around the room. When she came home to the Chinese Castle, (maybe more about that later), I pulled out my guitar and from the first strum of my guitar, I knew she could hear me. And, not long after that, she looked up at me and smiled, she stopped smiling when I withdrew and smiled at me again when I came close to her. She knew me; as did all of my children. So, when I saw that picture of the smiling baby, it reaffirmed what I had learned from fatherhood; most babies are not only cognitive of their surroundings, but their senses, although still developing, are not impaired when they are born. And that smile on that baby's face is not gas; it's pure, happiness to be with the ones that love and cherish them.

39

FOREVER FRIENDS

Ain't These Them Hard Times
Come To My Need
Forever Friends
After The Rain
Reluctant For Love
I know When It's Time To Leave
Those Golden Days
Just Fine
So Far To Go
Story Eyes
Forever Friends

40

Ain't These Them Hard Times (We Been Talking About)

Richie been looking all over the northwest
for work to keep his family out of debt.
Turned down, patronized and strung out like the rest,
because there's not too many paying jobs to get.
Bad back, complications, Ray's stuck in the mire.
Down to picking up river debris.
Take it home, chop it up, throw it on the fire,
one short step away from poverty.

Ain't these them hard times we been talking about
supposed to come some future year?
Better board up the windows and load up the guns,
hard times are finally here.

Standing in the food line with a rock churning in my gut,
for government cheese that's passed around.

Dignity and pride are eating at me but,
A man's gotta do something when he's down.
Taxes due, payments late and the bank at the door
the car's been repossessed and towed away.
Have to sell what I can, hope they don't ask for more,
I'm just barely getting by from day to day.

Ain't these them hard times we been talking about
supposed to come some future year?
Better board up the windows and load up the guns,
because hard times are finally here.

Coming down the wire,... seems it's every man for himself
trying to get that last slice of the pie,...
but what's to be done for everybody else
when the only store is burning in the night?
Seems like pretty soon, we're all heading for a war
over shelter, fuel and enough to eat.
Can't hardly trust the neighbors anymore,
just true friends and some family down the street.

Ain't these them hard times we been talking about
supposed to come some future year?
Better board up the windows and load up the guns,
because hard times are finally here.

41

Forever Friends

Just you and I, forever friends.
The way it all began,
the way it is in the end.
Forever love, just you and I,
so much road ahead,
so much road behind.
And it goes on past our view, to eternity.
And we go on, hand in hand to eternity.
We are forever, forever friends.
Just you and me, forever love.
So simple it seems,
but it's more than enough.
Forever friends, just you and me,
so much life gone by, so much left to see.
And it goes on past our view, to eternity.
And love goes on, hand in hand
to eternity.
We are forever, forever friends.

4 2

Come To My Need

Everywhere I turn I'm reminded of you,
even though our love is on hold because of you.
You want space to find yourself,
away from our war,
but I can't seem to get myself together anymore.
So, come on Honey stop this hesitation for me
I'm in trouble, come to my need.
Aimlessly I'm doomed to grope in search of true love,
but you don't seem to understand,
it's you I'm thinking of.
You say to search the field and look for somebody new,
but listen Babe, I'm strung out and only on you.
So, help me, I'm in way too deep, I'm in trouble, come to my need.
It's hard to put to words, all these feelings of mine,
yet I want to express all the good you've done in my life.
Our joining together has caused a change in what I am.
It was good to feel confidence
in a true and loving friend.
So please, consider what you seek, I'm in trouble, come to my need.
So tell me, how long will it be? I'm in trouble, come to my need.

43

After The Rain

After the rain, we'll get back to where we've been.
It's a brand-new dawn, to start over again.
After the rain, I can see for miles and miles.
as the warmth in a breeze brings out my best smiles.
Things always look brighter
and fresh again,
when the sun breaks through the clouds,
after the rain.
After the rain,

and the air is fresh and clean.
The sky is all blue, and the garden all green.
After the rain, rainbows dancing in the light.
Just like this day, I can start all over right.
Water rolls from the rooftops,
on down the drain,
then the sun breaks through the clouds,
after the rain.
After the rain,

skies open up, clouds disappear.
So much to see, and so much to do from here.
After the rain, all the choices are at hand.
I can still see the past, but now I understand.
Things always seem their darkest
till the storm finally breaks,
and the sun breaks through the clouds,
after the rain.

44

Reluctant For Love

Struggling so hard to find who I am.
Answers are riddles,
my faith is a sham,
my confidence sways.
I can't understand what all of this means,
I'm always confused, my future just seems
so distant and vague.

I don't want to live my life in loneliness;
Isolated and left all alone.
I don't want to live my life in loneliness,
but I'm so afraid, I just stay home.

Lost and unsure when a chance finally nears.
My heart full of hope,
but clouded by fears,
I'm reluctant for love.
I don't understand what makes me so shy,
afraid to be bold, afraid to just try
to reach out for love.

I'd like the same chance
for happiness to shine on me.
I can't continue like this,
but I don't know how to break free.

I don't want to live my life in loneliness
—isolated and left all alone.
I don't want to live my life in loneliness,
but I'm so afraid, I just stay home.

All of my life I thought there would be
some special person
out there for me
and knows what to do.
Ready for love, should it pass by my way
hoping I'll find the courage to say
I need you too.

45

I Know When It's Time To Leave

It's such a big joke,
the way you changed your mind.
All those words you spoke
were related to a different time.
But don't turn away like you're so naïve,
because I know when it's time to stay
and I know when it's time to leave.

You've gone out of your way
to avoid facing me.
Is it so hard to relate
to changes from what used to be?
I can't really say what I truly believe
but I know when it's time to stay,
and I know when it's time to leave.

I know about your friend
and the plans you've gone through.

If this is really the end,
I wish you could have told me too.
but you won't have to play
that ace up your sleeve,
I know when it's time to stay,
and I know when it's time to leave.

I take no promise to heart
and how could you miss?
Still I wish we'd part
on a different note than this.
But I'll be on my way by early eve
Babe, I know when it's time to stay,...
and I know when it's time to leave.

46

Story Eyes

Story eyes, mesmerizing,
losing my heart
yet realizing,
I love you,
I really do.
All my days are spent contemplating,
thinking of you
and our relations.
I love you,
I really do.
All my words fall short and slip away
in a million years
I could never say
what I feel.
So I'll spend my days in your sweet care,
always in love
and always there.
I love you,
you know I do.

47

Those Golden Days

All those golden days, they just keep on coming;
all those days, they just keep on running.
And me, I'm just getting closer to old.
That old man time doesn't care how it feels,
he is laughing at us while we're under his wheels.
Telling us, so we know
that there is no deals to be made.

I don't know where it went, like a ghost it went past.
I can't see how it all got spent, like a shadow it just didn't last.
Seems like only yesterday, I had so much time to play,
but now I'm rolling down this hill,
I Got no breaks to stand still.

All those silver words appear untarnished,
diamond photographs, all flower garnished
to keep the past well polished yet,
all those golden days, they just keep on coming,
all those days, they just keep on running,
And me,...

I'm just getting closer to old.

I still don't know where it went,
like a ghost it went past.
I can't see how it all got spent,
like a shadow it just didn't last.
Seems like only yesterday,
I had so much time to play,
now I'm rolling down this hill,
I Got no breaks to stand still.
And those golden days,
they just keep on coming
all those days, they just keep on running.
And me,...
I'm just getting closer to old.

48

Just Fine

When everything breaks down all around our lives.
It's hard to lose what's gone, to go on as it arrives.
But it's the nature of the changes that push us on in life.
We'll be alright, you'll see, things are going to be just fine.

As time goes on it seems, even memories fade away.
The friends we held so kind, had to find their day.
Although we yearn to have them closer,
once in a while we drop them a line,
and it's difficult to see, things are going to be just fine.

When the spirit seems gone, hard to go on day to day.
With directions all lost,
we have to find the cause and walk a better way.
As everything breaks apart, and your heart hurts from then.
It's hard to see beyond, to go on again.
But it's the nature of the changes that help us grow in life.
You'll be alright, you'll see, things are going to be just fine.

49

So Far To Go

We're on the moon, we touch the stars.
Traverse the planet in our cars.
Travel the skies, in jet speeds go,
exploring oceans miles below.
Yet we, in search to find our own,
get further from our natural home.
We've come so far—so much we know.
yet where we are, so far to go.

Our bounty great, reflecting days
of learning more productive ways.
Twice as much with half the land, a
nd hybrid chemicals close at hand.
Yet the third world, raped by greed
deprive the poor that stand in need.
We've come so far—so much we know,
yet where we are, so far to go.

Technology races with mankind,
while computers play the human mind.

Information, bought and sold
that we might all be "In The Know,"
won't substitute, only prolong
the ignorance of all the wrong.
We've come so far—so much we know,
yet where we are, so far to go.

Bureaucracies and governments,
all gamble on our environment.
From it all, we still can't see
we're killing off ourselves to be?
Our arrogance and stubborn gall
will sure enough destroy us all.
We've come so far—so much we know,
yet where we are, so far to go.

50

Forever Friends (Reprise)

Just you and I, forever friends.
The way it all began,
the way it is in the end.
Forever love, just you and I,
so much road ahead, so much road behind.
And it goes on past our view, to eternity.
And we go on, hand in hand to eternity.
We are forever, forever friends.

Just you and me, forever love.
So simple it seems, but it's more than enough.
Forever friends, just you and me,
so much life gone by, so much left to see.
And it goes on past our view, to eternity.
And love goes on, hand in hand to eternity.
We are forever, forever friends.

<h1 style="text-align:center">51</h1>

⟨◎❦⟩

MEMOIRS & NOTES - 03 - 'FOREVER FRIENDS'

Ain't These Them Hard Times (We Been Talking About)

(Written in 1984) – This is one of a few "Doomsday Propheteering" type songs that kind of heralded a need to keep a watch on the changing times. There were some hard times that hit the Baldwin Brothers and their families back in the late 70s and early 80s. This poem did document some of those things, like Richie, Ray and myself all being unemployed, or me standing in line to get government cheese, Ray, being disabled from an accident to his shoulder and back that he carries to this day; always in between settlements and being so broke one winter that Ray and his three boys would walk the back pasture of dad's farm picking up wood and debris leftover from the last river flood. There were bill collectors that hounded him at his home, and Richie had his beautiful car repossessed because he missed a few payments. Moreover, during the Carter recession years and especially during the mean-spirited Reagan years, there was a general feeling that the rich were getting richer at the expense and degradation of the poor, and seeing as how we were all in that situation of being poor, I would play this song and we would all empathize and commiserate with each other and the circumstances as Ray would reassure us through one of his many conspiracy theories, that they, (the government or the police or an establishment called "the New World Order"), were out to get us. But at least we had each other.

Come To My Need

(Written in 1984) – The lyrics from this song came from something Richie had said when we were both out in the barn cleaning stalls one weekend in 1984. It stuck in my head and that afternoon; I wrote down the words to the poem and the beginnings of what would be this song. The following Monday, I was at the funeral home waiting to speak to some family about arrangements and I sat at the old tube-set organ that was in the chapel grinding out the chords to the song. It was there that I changed the words to fit the changes in the music of the chorus, "I'm in trouble — come to my need."

Side Note:

In retrospect, this is kind of a weird relationship song as a love-war is going on and a truce is being asked for. He can't let her go, but he does expect her to come to him not the other way around. (*"Try to see it my way, only time will tell if I am right or I am wrong; while you see it your way, there's a chance that we might fall apart before too long,"* a reference to McCartney's relationship with Jane Asher with, *"We Can Work It Out."*

Forever Friends

(Written in 1991) – This sounded so good in my head when I created it and the message was strong, so I made the decision to name the album after it. The song didn't turn out to be as solid as I'd hoped. I think with a better three-part harmony and played in a different key, this song, about admonishing the importance and significance of a true friend, could still be something special.

After The Rain

(Written in 1990) – This was a quick, half-hour lunchtime song that tried to catch the feel of that fresh, clean ambiance after it rains, felt good, in spite of the little to no message value. It recorded well and sounded great. I tried to return to this song to tweak it a bit, but I never found what master it was recorded on and so, I moved on.

Side Note:

It was because of this missing song that I became somewhat obsessed with documenting what was on each four-track cassette and where it was on the tape.

Reluctant For Love

(Written in 1986-88) – After I left high school, and all through my lonely single life I thought that somewhere out there in that big world there was a special person looking and maybe dreaming of someone to come along like me. Like me, that person would be ready for the commitment and responsibility of love and companionship. And I felt, should the opportunity pass by my way, I would not only recognize that opportunity, but I would conquer my shyness, she might overcome hers, and together we would find a special commonality that we could build a lifetime relationship with.

Side Note:

Diane once confided in me that if I had not come along, she might not have gotten married and might even have spent her life living alone. Because I know her heart, I took that feeling — that possible quiet desperation and wrote these lyrics. I never told her about the correlation, nor do I think she has ever made any association, but I feel that the kind, goodness and sensitiveness of the character in the song shines through.

I Know When It's Time To Leave

(Written in 1991) – When I first played this song to Diane, her enthusiasm to the tune and lyrics motivated me to make this one of my performing pieces. And in public, this was well received. But this was one of those songs that was recorded, re-recorded and then re-recorded again, but because of the odd timing and syncopation, I could never truly capture the ambience or spirit of this piece. I think if I recorded this in a studio with other musicians the veracity and the energy of this song might be improved and shine through.

Those Golden Days

(Written in 1970-71) – In 1970-71 I was still just learning to play something more than 3-4 time on the piano, but let me shed some insight on what was happening at that time to me. I was living on the farm, which meant I was doing all the chores, meanwhile, I was going back and forth every day, with my dad, him going to work and me roaming around Portland looking for work. I could easily have gone back to working for Pratt's mortuary services, but that was a dead end where I slept all day and worked all night and there was no chance for upward mobility. **Maybe A Side Note:**

Back in Aurora there was a friend of Ray's named Tod, who, aside from a huge (and mostly unwarranted) ego that he needed feeding all the time, was also out of work, but he was not working at getting work. He made a casual, on-the-side living to get by, by selling stuff out of his parent's garage. In fact, I bought a Schwinn bike from him, supposedly his bike, for $25 dollars so he could buy a lid. Tod was also a budding musician with a capability of playing an elementary 4/4 timing. And after hearing some of my own rudimentary compositions, which had words to go with the songs, Tod sat down and flaunted his two, 4/4 tunes, both with catchy but mostly unmemorable lyrics. His playability over mine was noticeable and the knowing smile on his smug face caused me to want to compete with him, but I would need to move out of my comfort zone and practice. This song, "Golden Days" as well as reengineering an instrumental piece called, "Hollywood Heavens" were the songs that forced me to use different timings, different fingerings and different poetic meters to coincide with the music. It would seem that this song should have been written by someone after that person was closer to being in their Golden Years and after they'd experienced more of life and time's changes, than a young man of 22, but after I'd been talking to my dad, who, seeing his life going by quickly through the ever-changing windows of time, was complaining about how he never had time and how it just goes by so quickly — I wrote this song to reflect his age anxieties. So, every afternoon, after two o'clock, knowing that there was no need for jobhunting after two because most employers hire in the morning, infatuated with the go getters, I would head over to Portland State University and practice for two or three hours every day.

Side Note To Maybe A Side Note:

Fast forward a few months, I got a job working in a place called, Burger Chef and still carless, I was out with Ray when we stopped at Tod's house for a visit. The place was empty except for Tod, who greeted us and asked if we wanted a sandwich. Needing an injection into his ego, Tod led us to a baby grand piano in his folk's living room and began to play. He played both of his pieces (without much improvement from the last time I'd heard his stuff), and when he was done, he waited for the positive reinforcement he needed, which he got from both Ray and I. He then got up and started for the kitchen to make sandwiches. It was Ray who said that I had a new song that he should hear and so, with a note of annoyance, we went back to his piano. "Don't play anything to wild," Tod said, "They just had new strings put on this." I sat down, played "Golden Days" and without pausing, played, "Hollywood Heavens." Tod was speechless and dumbfounded. So much so, that Tod said that he'd forgotten that he had another pressing engagement and we ended up leaving. As we're driving towards Portland, Ray says, "We should a made the sandwiches before you played the piano."

Hollywood Heavens

(1970) – I was staying on the farm intermittently and one night on the news there was a story about how many of the studios and back-lots of Metro Golden Meyer were being sold off or destroyed. There was a quick glimpse of costumes and memorabilia that was being auctioned off to the public. But it was Dorothy's Ruby Slippers from, "The Wizard Of Oz," (still to this day, my favorite movie), that stirred something in my brain and caused me to compose this melody. This tune was always supposed to have lyrics, and many times when I played it, lyrics would come and go, but I never found the right words to match the emotions of the tune and so, it remained an instrumental.

Just Fine

(1991) – This was written for a coworker at the Washington State Parks department that I was acquainted with named Cindy, who was going through a lot of problems as a single parent. One day while I was passing, Cindy was crying because her life and relationships with her extended family and friends were a bit out of control. I sat with her as she poured out her problems to me and I felt compelled to tell her that things would be all right in a little while and that she should try to look beyond the turbulence and troubles of today and with forethought, towards a more forgiving tomorrow. That night I wrote the lyrics to this song and gave Cindy a copy of it the next day.

Side Note:

For the rest of the time that I worked at the Washington State Parks Department, Cindy honored me with having the poem taped and displayed on the wall of her office cubicle.

So Far To Go

(1991) – During George Bush Sr.'s Presidential term our ecological and environmental circumstances here in the United States as well as our interests in other countries were, to say the least, bleak. A year or so earlier, the tanker Exxon Valdez grounded on Bligh Reef in the upper part of Prince William Sound, spilling approximately 11 million gallons of crude oil that permeated everything. This problem was never resolved. Meanwhile, our country went to war, (Desert Storm) over Saddam Hussien taking control of Kuwait and its oil. Our technological advancements increased and we saw advancements everywhere explode from genetics to the newest generation of computer sciences with the 80386 processors (and 80486DX processors with a math coprocessor built in) And yet, the rich continued to have while the poor did without. And we'd come so far and yet, we had so far yet to go.

Side Note:

This song remains one of my top 25 songs to do live because I like the message, it feels good to sing and the chords are easy to traverse through. I look forward to rerecording this song at a later date.

Story Eyes

(1971) – This song was probably *conceived* before I met Diane, but as my piano works were improving, the song evolved and was refined to take on a greater meaning after I was dating Diane in 1971. At the time, I had no piano, and would buzz up to the piano practicing rooms at Portland State University to bang on the keys, practice new creations so as to create my songs. I had a very small repertoire at the time; this was one of those songs that developed from that era.

Side Note:

This was another one of the break-out songs that got me out of the ¾ time loop. It was difficult and I made a lot of mistakes. Maybe because I was conscientious of my inadequacies, or maybe it was because it was so personal, but this song was not a piece that I shared with others.

Forever Friends (Reprise)

(1991) – This second version of Forever Friends was a reprise of the earlier version, sung a cappella, (or acappella) in four-part harmony. I had visions of this version capturing a different feel to give variety to the piece, but I was still rather inexperienced at this craft. Again, it sounded good in my head when I created it and so I made the decision to do a return at the end of the album. The counterpoint and harmonies are interesting and although it too did not turn out to be as cool as I'd hoped, in my head I can still visualize something more striking with all the right voices interacting at the precise times they should. This would just need a little more time, but I was kind a hot to move to the next album and felt that this piece, would need to wait for some time tomorrow.

Side Note:

To be fair with my feelings of how complete my music was or was not, in those first years of recording, at first, after I got my four-track recording equipment, it was always my intention to get as much recorded as quickly as possible, so as to have a documentation, to be used to send out my material to record companies who, would see the brilliance of my stuff, however unpolished my material might be, after all, I'm a nobody, recording everything from my simple instruments and less-than entry-level recording equipment. And I felt that after I got better at the recording process and better with the piano, harmonica and guitar, I would return to revisit the best songs and then create a much better version. In reality, record companies and music contacts never panned out. There is a reason for that; record companies don't want to spend the time, money or energy listening to a nobody who did not pay to have his material recorded by professionals and even then, (at least back in the 80s and 90s) there was a divided division on what medium they wanted – reel-to-reel of cassette and if you sent the wrong format, whoosh, off it went into the trash. Frankly, even if you sent the right format, 99% of all material still ended up in the trash. And I spent a lot of money I didn't have to buy cassettes, special cassette envelopes and a secondary self-addressed, cassette envelope, with stamps and even a small note card where the listener can check boxes to let me know when the cassette was returned so I could get a feel for what they wanted. Out of the seventy or eighty cassettes that sent out, none ever came back.

5²

04 - SOMETHING MUST BE WRONG - 1992

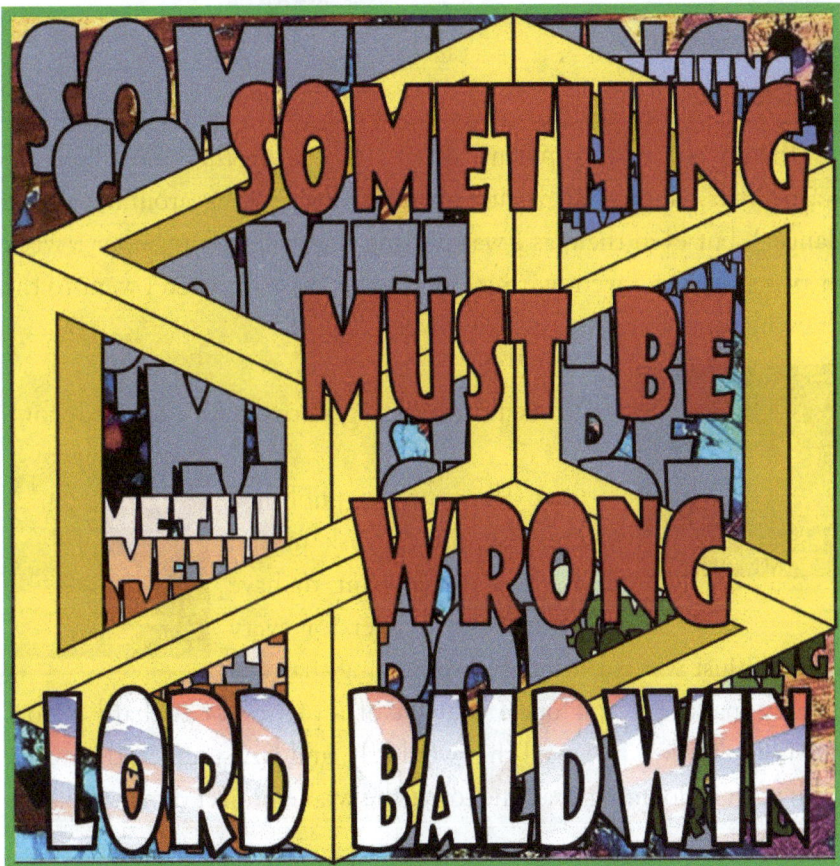

53

NOTES ABOUT THE COVERS:

There was a rush to put my original cover together and I honestly wasn't that happy with what I used, (a dog looking around, sensing danger), but even then, as I was putting these albums together a week or two at a time, I went with it. So, it was a blessing when I went to the drawing room to create the new cover.

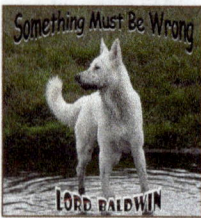

To be frank, getting all the WAV files ready for

each album to get published was a monumental task in and of itself, I didn't want to have to create a new cover for every album, I just wanted to plug in something that was already made. For this one I thought of a picture of Richard Nixon, but I didn't know how well that would fly, and last summer, that other push with its looming deadline to get the whole project done was hassle enough.

Using MS Word and the WordArt function, I started with the original picture of the dog, and pasted the title's words, "something must be wrong" and played with different fonts, sizes, shapes and colors, I even morphed and copied the words over the top of themselves in different sizes so that it repeated things, but I was never satisfied with the results. I decided to gray out most of the lettering and using the Showcase Gothic font and red lettering, I put the, "Something Must Be Wrong" on top of all the other letterings, but I didn't love it.

Just when it seemed I was going to have to let it be and send it to print, I found an Escher Cube, kind of like one that you might see in a Mad Magazine, then turned it yellow, to contrast with the red lettering and made it big enough to touch all four sides of the album cover. I then moved the red lettering on top or in front, and moved the red lettering around till you could see the cube's impossibility behind the lettering, then I put my name on it and called it good.

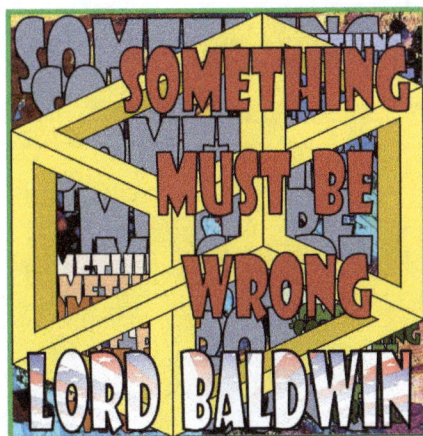

54

SOMETHING MUST BE WRONG

Something Must Be Wrong
You're So Smart
When You Touch My Heart
Somewhere In Between
Something For Myself
Worried
Tumbleweed
Flapjack Mama
Rolling In The Clover
I Am The Fool
Who's In Charge Of It All
"Something Must Be Wrong,"

55

Something Must Be Wrong

Went to the drugstore to get a newspaper and a coke,
I walked back home, did the crossword puzzles and read the jokes.
Then I come in here and there you are on the box,
and I just turn you off because I'm all alone.
Something must be wrong if we can't seem to communicate.
Something must be wrong if all you ever do is hate.
Something must be wrong if you don't feel the things you do,
Something must be wrong, something must be wrong,
something must be wrong with you.

Hopped in my car to get a pizza and a burger when
I started running out of gas and I had to walk back home again.
Then I come in here and there you are on the floor
and you ask me if I'm sore but sure I can't take this anymore.
Something must be wrong if we can't see eye to eye.
Something must be wrong if all you ever do is lie.
Something must be wrong if you don't feel the things you do,
Something must be wrong, something must be wrong,
something must be wrong with you.

Went to the doctor's to see if he might help,
he said, "You better go back home boy, and get into your bed."
So, I'm walking home slow, feeling kind of low,
then I see you ripped the sheets of the bed
and yanked out the phone.
Something must be wrong if you can't tell me where you've been.
Something must be wrong with you cheating on me again.
Something must be wrong if you don't feel the things you do,
Something must be wrong, something must be wrong,
something must be wrong with you.

56

You're So Smart

You're so smart,
you finally got things to go your way.
Didn't give her room for a single word to say.
You directed it all like some dramatic play.
Orchestrated to such a fine art, you're so smart.

You're so smart, you made her take the heavy part of a fool.
Twisting words around and changing all the rules.
Standing your ground, acting so cool.
She was so helpless as you tore her all apart, you're so smart.

You're so wise, to think that she believed in all your lies.
You're so right, that's why you sit alone here tonight.

You're so smart,
to give the silent treatment to your best friend,
to make it too hard for her to make amends.
You got the house all to yourself again.
And it was so easy for you to break her heart,
you're so smart.

57

When You Touch My Heart

So much to say, so much to relate, so little time.
We all fight the same disease of loneliness inside.
We're all on this great big planet, millions of people there,
trying to touch a heart to show all that they care.
The moment is special, as charity overcomes the strife.
Unselfish persons reaching out to share their lives.
Sorrow is gone, instead, hope for the day to share,
when you touch my heart to show me that you care.
Skies grow dark, foreboding, rain falls when should be fair.
People, apprehensive run for shelter everywhere.
And still you reach out, to untangle me in my snare,
when you touch my heart to show me that you care.
Sometimes the risk is great, sometimes the faith is gone,
and its hard to know the right directions to go on.
But you seize the wild chances, willing to take the dare,
when you touch my heart and show me that you care.
So much to say, so much to relate and so little time.
We all share the same disease of loneliness inside.
You know the cure, my love, you know it's always there,
when you touch my heart to show me that you care.

58

Somewhere In Between

Arguments won't solve the problems
and these feelings need to cease.
What we both want can't be met, but what we need is peace.
In your mind, you think you're right
while I want to follow my dream,
there must be a way we both can feel good somewhere in between.
All this distance separating us
just proves the point that it should.
But Honey, it's not really doing either of us any good.
Seems to me, it's a no-win game, that's all it's ever been.
Maybe a solution lies somewhere in between.
Our lines are drawn for battle though the area is mostly gray.
Is the risk of gaining vantage worth throwing everything away.
Should we continue with attitudes one-sided crass and mean?
Or, could we surrender and seek a truce somewhere in between.
You can close your mind and then your heart
while I sting my words at you.
but can't you see the end results is tearing us both in two.
I'd like to put this all behind us and start all over clean.
live within the compromise somewhere in between.

59

Something For Myself

All this anger I hold is no fault of theirs,
and what of good deeds with a heart in repairs?
I look out at my life and I know it's right,
and yet, there's something missing inside.

It's three steps forward and two steps back.,
not a whole lot of progress, but I'm on the right track.
I've spent my whole day helping everybody else,
it's time I did something for myself.

Nothing wrong with losing self in things you do,
but there comes a time to do it for you.
I'm not saying to be selfish, or to do just for me,
but I'm not meeting up to my own needs.

It's three steps forward and two steps back.
Not a whole lot of progress, but I'm on the right track.
I've spent my whole day helping everybody else,
it's a time I can do something for myself.

All this anger you hold is no fault of theirs,
and what of good deeds with your heart in repairs?
You look at your life and must know it's right,
and yet, there's something missing inside.

It's three steps forward and two steps back.
Not a whole lot of progress, but you're on the right track.
You've spent your whole day helping everybody else,
it's time you did something for yourself.

60

Worried

I worry for the future of ecology's lot.
I worry about why, and I worry why not.
I worry about my children; do they get enough?
I worry about my children; do they get too much?
I'm worried, worried, worried, worried.

I'm worried about the time that moves too fast,
I'm worried about the present catching up with my past.
I worry my teeth and my hair falling out,
I worry about our food with all these chemicals about.
I worry, worry, I worry, worry.

Got to stop, too much stress to take.
Always dwelling in doubt is a big mistake.
Got to stop being a worry slave,
or I'll worry myself to an early grave.

I'm worried about the economy falling into the night,
I worry about world leaders doing what's right.
I worry about my friends and how they might be,

I worry about my friends and what they think of me.
And I'm worried, worried, worried, worried.

I'm worried about the air with every breath,
I'm worried about life and worried about death.
I worry did my life have something to tell.
I'm worried about heaven and I'm worried about hell.
I worry, worry; I worry, worry.

Got to stop, too much stress to take.
Always dwelling in doubt is a big mistake.
Got to stop being a worry slave,
or I'll worry myself to an early grave.

61

Tumbleweed

See the birds winging over the bay,
I can't go, but you can't stay, my Love.
Winter winds are whispering your name,
you've no want to stay that game and follow.
So fly away, fly away my Love.
Long goodbyes, like the leaves turning brown,
too many words to explain the down
we're both feeling.
I can't stand to watch you die,
I know how these winters bring sorrow.
I can't cage the fire in your eyes,
as you gaze down that road for tomorrow.
So, fly away, fly away my Love.
You're a tumbleweed, growing roots in the fall
to roll to the south
as summer winds call you to roll.
Cars are calling from the highway of dreams,
your lifeblood is pulling
you back in its stream so go.
and fly away, fly away my Love.

62

Flapjack Mama

Flapjack Mama, living in Packwood City,
slapping them greasy tatters down on hot plates.
She says, "I ain't no hash slinger, I ain't no hash slinger,
I'm a public accountant, sometimes, a dental assistant".
Flapjack Mama, working in Packwood City,
flapping them cakes, graveyard shift, all night.
She says, "I got the number here, I've got an inside,
I'm just a little overweight and too old to be a model".
Flapjack Mama, waiting in Packwood City,
cleaning up the back and waiting for Randy's return.
Randy's been up in the mountains,
and he's coming home with candy
to his two-hundred-and-fifty-pound baby,
Randy don't care.
Flapjack Mama, dreaming in Packwood City,
holding down a waitress & cook's job at the same time.
She says, "Someday I'll own this hole in the wall,
someday me and Randy will be set for a family,
gonna retire if I don't."
Flapjack Mama, Flapjack Mama, Flapjack Mama.

63

Rolling In The Clover

Burn the oil lamps late tonight.
I've got a feeling that is holding to me tight.
My mind was reeling at a fantastic flight.
I felt the presence and I saw the light
I'm rolling in the clover, knowing that it's all over.
Hoping that in the end, you'll be my friend.
Second looks at idol time to seed,
realization that I had all that I need.
answers of the balance, everything in simple terms
how much did I love, and how much did I learn?
I'm rolling in the clover, knowing that it's all over.
Hoping that in the end, you'll be my friend.
All my life was shown before my eyes,
all my days of truth and all my times of lies.
Though at time, I was wrong, at times I almost fell.
All in all, still I know I balanced out quite well,
and I'm rolling in the clover,
knowing that it's all over, now.
Hoping that in the end, you'll be my friend.

64

I Am The Fool Who's In
Charge Of It All

There is no hidden reason for this sad falling away,
the fault is all mine. I take all the blame.
With nowhere else to go, nobody else to call,
I am the fool who's in charge of it all.

I shouldn't be surprised; she doesn't want me to return.
My bridges are still blazing from the fires I left burn.
I hurt her, she left me, now I'm stuck with my own gall,
and I am the fool who's in charge of it all.

I think how could she hurt me just because I am a lout,
but then again, where was my head
when I let that girl walk out?

With my pig head too thick, I wouldn't try to see her side,
I must have pushed her too far, always needing to be right.
Pretending I didn't need her;
high and mighty, strong and tall,

now I am the fool who's in charge of it all.

I'd like her to know my changes, since we've been apart,
but just saying I'm sorry won't heal a broken heart.

Still sulking from my wrong approach to this fight,
wondering if there is ever any way to make things right.
Mistakes and short-comings caused my whole world to fall,
I am the fool who's in charge of it all.

65

MEMOIRS & NOTES -04- 'SOMETHING MUST BE WRONG'

Something Must Be Wrong

(Written in 1974) – This is one of my old standby pieces that I like to play when I need to warm people up and get them going. It holds double meanings, one, as a reflection of Senior, my stepfather of 12 years, and the other as Nixon. In early 1974 there was a lot of trouble brewing for our not-so-good President,... Richard M. Nixon. I would see his face on television every night and by summer, the whole Watergate circus was in full session. I originally wrote the words to this poem because I was getting tired of seeing his face and hearing his hollow words. On Aug. 9, 1974, Nixon resigned his office and was succeeded by Vice-President Gerald R. Ford who, a month after Nixon's resignation, pardoned him for the crimes he committed as president. After seeing Nixon sheepishly (and wrongfully) accept the pardon, I momentarily felt sorry for him and altered the words of this poem to reflect a kind of, love-gone-bad scenario. Later on, after Nixon sought to portray himself as an elder statesman, I kind of mixed the two and that is how this poem remains to this day.

Side Note:

This song should have been on one of the first two albums, but after I recorded the song early on, I felt it lacked the drive and energy that I seemed to achieve while playing it live, so although I recorded the piece, it got shelved to become part of this 4th album.

You're So Smart

(Written in 1991) – I got into an argument with Diane about who knows what and after I drove my point home leaving her no room for compromise or posturing, she left the room with the resulting statement, "you're so smart." So, there's this man that is sitting alone in a deserted living room retracing his steps, while he can hear the faint sounds of his best friend crying in the back room. So, I realized that my winning caused a division in our relationship resulting in me actually losing, and having the last word can be satisfying for a fleeting moment, but the consequence of that cold and cruel outcome was and is not to my liking nor in my quest to be right, was it my desired result. And so, I wrote this poem to document and point out and remember that contrasting opinions can cause an opposition or a clash and or a separation from what you wanted.

When You Touch My Heart

(Written in 1991) – I was in the lunchroom at the State Parks one day talking to some of the other women workers there. The subject of single parents and their needs came up and the talk went on and on focusing on their (the single women's) problems dating and relationships and I, trying to include myself in the conversation said, "We all share the same disease of loneliness inside." From this one statement, which I wrote down almost immediately on an unforgiving napkin, this poem was born. Realizing that love, that true special love, can be motivated and obtained with the simplest of kind acts by just showing that you care. I stayed late after work that night and put the lyrics together adding, "When you touch my heart" to the chorus line.

Side Note:

At the time I had this tune I was messing around with on the guitar, and I just put these new words with that tune and there you have it, it worked wonderfully. Sometimes the marriage of words and music are so exquisite that I wonder how it happens. This was one of those fusions—and again, one of the songs that didn't quite make it to the first two albums.

Somewhere In Between

(Written in 1983) – After working at the funeral home for a while and interacting with the managing funeral director, Gary Rook, I started to understand what it was I was doing, and in the process, I started to believe in myself and my abilities as a writer and musician. Also, because I was exposed to Mr. Rook's extensive vocabulary, my own vocabulary increased. This whole experience opened up new channels and insights for my songwriting and my writing block disappeared. I experimented with a lot of subjects and ideas and was writing lyrics about everything that sounded good to me at the time. I was driving to work one morning, annoyed after having had an argument with Diane.

Side Note:

During a cooling down period at work, I analyzed the incidence and tried to look at the problem or argument from both sides, the give and take, the cooperation or lack thereof, the negotiations, the compromises, and how we could come to some type of reconciliation. I wrote down my feelings and observations of the occurrence. In between funeral services, my voice echoed through the empty funeral home chapel as I composed the music on the organ in there. That night I played it for Diane when I got home and felt it was a good song after she started crying.

Something For Myself

(Written in 1991) – This woman I knew from the Wash. State Parks Dept., I think her name was Terry, explained how she spent the weekend taxiing her children from one activity to another, sometimes having to deal with simultaneous events with their varied scheduling conflicts and how it sometimes drove her crazy. She asked me if I thought it would be okay for her to tell her kids that the following Friday, she wanted to go, by herself, to a movie, (What About Bob), just to get away, relax, and let the responsibilities hold off for another day. She was asking me for my permission for her to take a day off. I said, "You should do something for yourself. Then you'll feel that it's alright to do stuff with them." Then I tried to represent that thought or concept from that happening through the lyrics.

Worry

(Written in 1991) – I was thinking about all the things I was worried about and sat down to document this huge list, ranging from personal health to the political affairs of the United States. I was really amazed at all the junk in my head slowing down or effecting my karma. I think that after I finally got this song out I was somewhat sedated or maybe insulated for a time from my problematic (neurotic) maybe even psychosomatic fears. The words in this poem kind of reflects a hypochondriac with a thanatophobia as well as psychosomatic tendencies, worried about everything as he compiles and confronts the small fears that plague and nag me in the back of my mind. And although I do worry about far too much and about things I can't change or even do anything about, arguably many of my worries are justifiable about things I should be concerned about, and so, I continue to worry.

Tumbleweed

(Written in 1968) – This song was actually conceived and toyed with in 1968 on a friend's piano in Brown's Mills, New Jersey. I played the tune (without words) during the summer of 1968 as well as on the weekends in the fall of that year within varied cocktail lounges or mini-bars located all over the Concord Hotel in Upstate, New York. There was no shortage of baby-grand pianos there and I would sneak into the hotel, find one of the places with an open piano and start playing. Many of the bartenders got to know me and some of them liked what I did. Arguably, I wasn't that good, but when you're playing in a dimly lit room to a bunch of drunks that thrive on my type of emotional music, things had a way to even things out. One time I was even asked if I wanted a job playing piano for the guests by the head recreational coordinator for the hotel. I told him I only did my own material and he smiled and said, "Maybe later."

Side Note:

The second half of my senior year was spent in a small high school out in Donald, Oregon called North Marion High School. Because I had moved around so much and attended so many different schools, my transcripts were all screwed up. When I arrived, I was informed that I had too many credit years of PE and not enough math. So, I had to double up on math classes and I had two days a week where I had an hour to do nothing. I arranged with the choir teacher (Mrs. Clapp) to be let into the music room so I could play around on the piano. It was during one of those hours that I finally composed the words to the poem and music for this poem.

Flapjack Mama

(Written in 1977) – In the seventies I was an avid mountain climber. Not to the degree as some of my friends, but I was in the Pacific Northwest where there are many mountains; Mt Hood in Portland, Mt Adams, Mt St. Helens, Mt. Baker and Mt Rainier to name a few. I had friends that went up to the mountains every 3 or 4 day weekend, and a wonderful wife that encouraged me to go along. One morning, about 2 AM, with my friends Cliff and Randy, we stopped into this small diner in Packwood, Washington on our way to Mt. Rainier. This little hash house/truck stop was about the only thing open and we were all hungry. The waitress there was this tall, heavy-set woman that had a few teeth missing from her smile, but seemed genuinely pleased that we stopped in. When she came over to the table to take our orders, she was particularly interested in Randy, who normally had no interest in girls. The place was shorthanded that night so she was holding down the cook's job and waitress job at the same time, and in between grilling our food, she walked back and forth, getting real friendly with Randy. She told us that she was working many different jobs at the same time. She took some verbal liberties about a supposed relationship between her and Randy.

When Randy jokingly displayed some interest in her, they exchanged phone numbers and she alluded to a get-together after her shift got done later that morning. She was sitting in our booth, next to Randy as we ate our food and afterwards, gave Randy his food for free. All that weekend we joked about Randy's new girl friend in Packwood City. At the end of the weekend, we even stopped in to see her, but she wasn't there. The cook said he thought she was working down in Randle, at a dentist's office.

Rolling In The Clover

(1968) – This is another one of the songs that I played in the cocktail lounges at the Concord Hotel. I had words written down on sheets of paper and looked like I was reading music. Not having a large repertoire, I played this song often because I could play it well. Too often, sometimes three or four times a night. The guests didn't seem to mind, but some of the bartenders did. There were times I would be asked to leave, so I'd take my papers and walk downstairs to another bar and do this song again. The lyrics have evolved over the years, but the essence of what this song was about, still shines through.

I Am The Fool Who's In Charge Of It All

(1982-83) – After finalizing the funeral arrangements for a 40-year-old man that accidentally died in his bathtub, his mother, who was in her late 60s, asked me to come over to her place to sign the paperwork. When I got there, she had a bunch of his stuff in the living room and asked me to take what I wanted and give the rest to Goodwill. There was a trumpet and a cheap guitar that I thought might be good to give to the kids. (This trumpet, that we still have, was used in school by Chet, Lori, Ben, Stephen and Spencer). I took the guitar to work and hid it inside one of the caskets in the display room (the Cherrywood). Although the guitar was beat up and the frets were a bit off, I was in this creative period and sometimes inspiration needed me to do things then and there. I was strumming these blues chords when the song popped out at me.

Side Note:

Inspired by Merle Haggard's Misery and Gin from the Bronco Billy movie, I thought I'd write a song that Merle might like. It became an instant hit with my family, especially Meridith, who, at the time was about 4 or 5, remembered the words and sang the song all the time.

66

❧

05 - IT WASN'T MY FAULT

- 1992

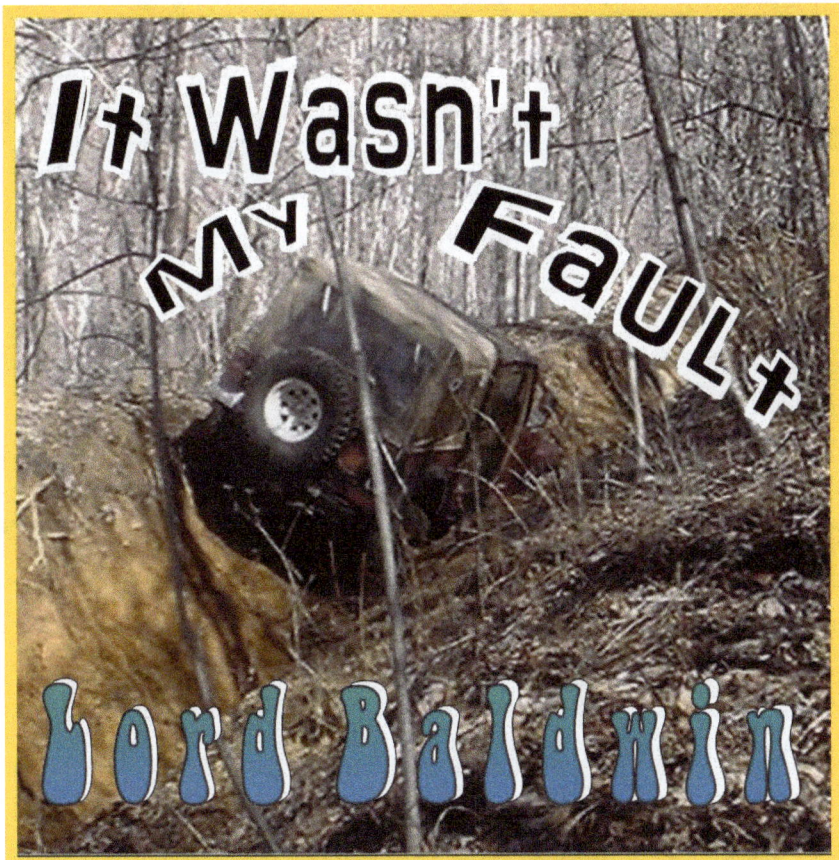

67

NOTES ABOUT THE
COVERS:

As before mentioned, there was a rush to put my covers together, but I felt this cover was good and I wouldn't be called on it by the publisher, and I was happy with what I had.

There were problems, the document that I imported the original cover from 1992

was created using Word Perfect, and the conversion to MS Word in 2002 was not kind to the original and I was not able to carry over the original fonts, and in those days, I was known as Lord Chester L. Baldwin II.

I believe it was my friend Trudi that coined the shortened new name and pseudonym, Lord Baldwin.

So, using MS Word and the WordArt function, I used the quirky, AR DARLING font for the title, It Wasn't My Fault, and Bell Bottom.Laser font for my name; Lord Baldwin.

68

IT WASN'T MY FAULT

It Wasn't My Fault
Two Dollars Short
But I Changed My Mind
I Been There Before
Early Morning Sun
Dream Your Troubles
Crazy Cars
Forget-Me-Nots
How Does One?
All The Man I Was
Down The Road

69

It Wasn't My Fault

While playing my guitar in the park one day,
an audience had gathered and was listening to me play.
We were all having a good time,
till the bikers caused fear to fall.
They were throwing rocks and punches
and it turned into a brawl.

But it wasn't my fault, it wasn't my fault,
I was only trying to sing my songs.
It wasn't my fault, it wasn't my fault,
Why is it everybody comes to me
when something goes wrong.

We were trying to be helpful to a friend down on his luck,
so friends and family pitched in to buy him a used truck.
He was hauling pigs to market
as a squirrel ran across the street,
he crashed the truck, killed the pigs,
and the creditors came looking for me.

But it wasn't my fault, it wasn't my fault,
I was only trying to help the guy along.
It wasn't my fault, it wasn't my fault,
Why is it everybody comes to me
when something goes wrong.

Now many of you people as you leave from here tonight,
might feel a bit uneasy, maybe you don't feel quite right.
Then you think back on this evening
and the tickets that you bought,
but please don't blame the music
for the sickness you've now got.

Hey, because it wasn't my fault, it wasn't my fault,
I was only trying to sing my songs,
It wasn't my fault, it wasn't my fault,
Why is it everybody comes to me
when something goes wrong.

70

Two Dollars Short

It was many years ago, I was traveling the Northern roads.
I got stranded and broke down in a small Montana town.
I phoned home to help me out and stayed at a halfway house,
that was trying to save my soul
till my money arrived from my folks.
It was there I first saw him sit, half serious and half lit.
Singing songs of Michael's boat
with a bottle concealed in his coat.
He looked at me with eyes from the grave,
through a face badly needing a shave.
We talked of his life living alone,
and I remember his words like my own,

He said, "Now I see, your ways differ from me,
but I must overcome my fears
that's why I'm sitting here getting drunk on this port.
And I know, there's a better road, but I ain't found it yet
and this is all you get when you're two dollars short."

Through years that swiftly ran, I forgot all about that man.

Then one day I was thrown in jail and he was there inside my cell.
Picked up for a vagrant bum, they were holding him for the run.
Once again, we talked for hours
till the dawn shown through the bars.

He said, "Now I see, your ways differ from me,
but I must overcome my fears
that's why I'm sitting here to be arraigned in this court.
And I know, there's a better road, but I ain't found it yet
and this is all you get when you're two dollars short."

After breakfast came along, I sensed something was wrong.
the old man fell on the floor and stopped moving by the door.
As they were taking him to intensive care,
they let me out to go with him there.
In the ambulance he tried to tell me once more before he died.

He said, "Now I see, your ways differ from me,
but I must overcome my fears
that's why I'm dying here with no family to support.
And I know, there's a better road, but I ain't found it yet
and this is all you get when you're two dollars short."

At his funeral alone I stood, and I thought,
"what a shame for a man so good
to have done all the things he did, yet kept his talents hid."
I tried to correlate between his and my own fate,
it didn't take long to see, that he was an awful lot like me.

Now I see, what I can come to be, if I don't overcome my fears
I'll just go year to year without any better resort.
And I know, there's a better road, and I will find it yet
or else all I will get is just two dollars short.

71

But I Changed My Mind

It would have been a sure thing, and I would have been on the road,
to leave and get away as far as I could go.
Because we parted company, I left the past heretofore.
Thinking we'd never want to try our love together anymore.
But I changed my mind, had a change of heart
I've had such a hard time since we've been apart.
And since our love's turned bad,
contentment's hard to find.
You were the best thing I ever had, so, I changed my mind.
I thought it would be different than this,
but the truth is starting to unfold.
Without your spark of warm light, my life is empty and cold.
Didn't intend to make amends,
when I broke up our happy home.
I thought that I'd get over you, planned to live life alone.
But I changed my mind, had a change of heart
I've had such a hard time since we've been apart.
And since our love's turned bad, contentment's hard to find.
You were the best thing I ever had, so, I changed my mind.

72

I Been There Before

I played out my hand, cashed in my chips,
I relaxed my stand and let go of my grip.
I ended up alone, what we had became undone.
All she wanted was a home but I needed to run.
So I walked out that door, I been there before.

Aimed the car straight for Bend, but it was really hard to go.
The Lady's still in my head and I still love her so.
She'd have me working steady, coming home to cooked meals.
Always loving and ready to be concerned how I feel.
But She'd want so much more, I been there before.

She'd want lots of kids I'd say, maybe ten before we're through.
She'd support me all the way and believe in everything I do.
If I was down and sick, she'd nurse me back to health again,
and not complain a lick on how her hardship might have been.
But I really know what's in store, I been there before.

Am I running from the truth that I'm too afraid to see,
or hiding from true love that could endure for her and me?

It's no wonder I am cautious with apprehensions and doubts,
I've been hurt by other women, set up and cleaned out.

I played out my hand, but this game isn't through.
I don't know where I stand, and I don't know what to do.
Should I call her and say, "I was wrong, let's try again,"
or should I just walk away because I was hurt way back when?
But then what am I living for, to be lonely forever more,
I know love can be so much more,...
I been there before.

73

Early Morning Sun

Wake up, rub my eyes, greet the brand-new day.
Feel all the life around me,
hear the things they say.
Too much is going on to stay the sleepy one,
I need to get out there
in the early morning sun.
Sunrise is so unique with the colors in the sky.
A brand new day to start
discovering what and why.
I've got too much to do to spend lost, on the run.
I'm taking my sweet time
for the early morning sun.
Let go of yesterday, it's all but learned and gone.
The good chance to start again
is like this brand-new dawn.
It feels like the shining hope for good works to be done.
I need this dose of joy
from the early morning sun.

74

Dream Your Troubles To Sleep

Dream your troubles to sleep, little one.
You can dream of all the things you need.
When the sun decides to break, that's the time for you to wake,
until then you must sleep.
Close your eyes. Slowdown time, slumber is forming
and we need rest in life,
and you'll feel fine in the morning.
Please, no more whys, all your sighs are lost in the yawning.
Sleep, close your eyes, let the night take you to the dawning.
Dream your troubles to sleep, little one.
You can dream of all the things that you seek.
When the sun decides to break, that's the time for you to wake,
until then you should sleep.
Close your eyes. Slowdown time, slumber is forming
and we need rest in life, and you'll feel fine in the morning.
Please, no more whys, all your sighs are lost in the yawning.
Sleep, close your eyes, let the night take you to the dawning,
and sleep.

75

Crazy Cars

Crazy cars, crazy cars,
driving much too fast, drinking down the gas,
and like this it just can't last for those crazy cars.
Crazy cars, crazy cars
seem to have lost the art,
they don't build them anymore with their heart.
They just slap them together and they fall apart,
you gotta work all day just to make them start,
them old crazy cars.
Crazy cars, crazy cars
The M.P.G. is just below eleven,
gas going up to a dollar eighty-seven,
and with prices like that
to walk to work sure would be heaven
then driving them old crazy cars.
Crazy cars, crazy cars
and the highway man just ain't fair,
he'll take your land and won't give you a fair share,
and he can build a road almost anywhere
for them old crazy cars.

76

Forget-Me-Nots

In the window sill, soft and gentle blue,
waiting patiently to remind anew,
Forget-Me-Nots.
Soft and comforting, please remember me.
Shining in the flowers, promising what's ours,
Forget-Me-Nots.
So many small flowers, yet such brilliant blue.
So many small reasons for my love for you.
Thousands of pedals in just these few pots,
blooming like our love,
Forget-Me-Nots.
Touching quietly, the special heart,
the hopeful prayer, we will never part,
Forget-Me-Nots.
In the window sill, soft and gentle blue,
waiting patiently to remind anew,
Forget-Me-Nots,
Forget-Me-Nots.

77

How Does One

How does one find peace of mind
while life seems all amiss?
When can one believe again that they might rise from this?
Where can one reach out beyond,
if no winds grace their sails?
Will they ever see themselves as more than one who fails?
Where do I go now, after everything has turned sour?
The shame will pass, the hurt may leave,
but when it's changed, where will I be?
How does one forgive himself after failing in the test?
Where is the road of shaded trees
that a soul might find some rest?
Where do I go from here, after the sorrow and tears?
Time heals all wounds, the trials will fade,
but how do I get through today?
When does failure turn around so dreams of hope might start?
Where is love, where is God,
and does he know my heart?

78

All The Man I Was

Quickly runs my fleeting days, too soon time slips away.
Except for my beliefs held close,
my life will ebb and fade.
I would not follow blindly, doing what he says or does,
I stand for what I am from all the man I was.
This old and tired body has paid time's ageless debt.
All I ever believed in I carry with me yet.
No compromise is given,
standing firm and strong because
my heart and mind and spirit hold to all the man I was.
As all this life will soon leave, an end brings me no fear.
I need no words of praise to take my essence off from here.
It matters little if I'm thought of
with anguish or deep love
I only hope they see the strength in all the man I was.
My name my reputation,
the respect I gained through worth
My sense of honored conduct is what I leave this earth.
Material things come and go, just as the body does.
In a legacy of integrity shines all the man I was.

79

Down The Road

Too many times, the promises are strong,
but I can only hold on for so long,
then I'm going, going, gone, down the road.
I do my best, get strong, get tough
but sometimes even that is not enough
and I'm going, going, gone, down the road.
When a man decides it must be time to go,
even while he's working, he's halfway down the road
and I'm going, going, gone, down the road.
Thought I had a foothold solid as a stone,
but the bottom fell out and left me here all alone
so I'm going, going, gone, down the road.
I thought of staying out of loyalty or fear,
but there's really nothing left to keep me here
and I'm going, going, gone, down the road.
Don't know if I'm strong enough to fail or lose,
don't know where I'm heading,
but I'm free enough to choose
so I'm going, going, gone, I'm going, going, gone,
I'm going, going, gone, down the road.

80

⁂

MEMOIRS & NOTES - 05 - 'IT WASN'T MY FAULT'

It Wasn't My Fault

(Written in 1983) – Although I finished writing this piece in 1983, it had been kicking around in my head for over ten years. One Sunday summer afternoon in 1972 around 2, I went by bus up to the Washington Park in Northwestern Portland. I had made arrangements to meet Ray there and we were going to jam on guitars.

I was sitting on a grassy hillside just below some swing sets and outdoor toys, playing guitar and grooving with a small group of stoners. In less than a minute a large motorcycle group loudly pulled up, parked in the road just below us and then came up the hill and sat down. They seemed to expect me to entertain them so I played on. At the time I had only a small repertoire of songs and sheepishly strummed and joked around for most of the rest. These bikers had no sooner sat down when a couple of them just pulled out some weed and started smoking right there. I felt a bit intimidated and scared and kept hoping Ray would suddenly pull up in his little red MG, but he never arrived.

What did arrive was a couple police cars that cruised by, giving the bikers their evil eye as they passed. After they drove out of sight, this one big guy stood up and said, "Now I'm Bummed out!" to the rest of his gang and as the police drove by again, (and we all knew they would), he stood up and walked down towards the police car and said, "Do you want something?" to the policeman that was looking up at the group. The first police car stopped, followed by the police car behind it. No lights or sirens or warnings occurred, but instead I watched as one of the policemen got on the radio. I just knew I didn't want to see how this was going to end. As the two police got out of the first car carrying nightsticks, heated words were exchanged and I quickly grabbed my guitar and walked the other way, up and over the hill, joined with most of the stoners who didn't want any part of this eventual confrontation. I kept walking right out of the park and down back streets to avoid getting picked up for whatever. As I reached Burnside, I saw two police cars with their lights flashing quietly flying up the road towards the place I had just left. I heard from my friend Louie the next day that there was a rumble in the park and I filled him in on my end of the rest of the story.

Two Dollars Short

(Written in 1980) – In the early spring of 1970, after months of frustration, hopelessly looking for a job in Portland, I decided to hitch hike to the Catskills and see if I could get a station as a waiter for Passover. I left April 1, on a Wednesday night, to give me lots of time to get to New York before Passover which was April 11, but started in the hotels on the tenth. I decided to go up into Canada and then go across, over the top of the great lakes and come back down through northern New York and then down to Kiamesha Lakes.

Unfortunately, I got stuck for three days and nights at some cross-roads just outside of a city in Saskatchewan called Medicine Hat. By now it was Tuesday the 7th and I was running out of time. (More on this in "On The Open Road" Memoirs & Notes). I hitch hiked back down into the states and into Billings Montana where I called my dad and had him wire me $50.00 via Western Union so I could catch a plane.

The soonest I could catch a flight out to New York City was Thursday morning so I made arrangements to stay at the Salvation Army for the next two nights. It was there that I met Mr. Paul. I first saw him sitting to the left of me, dispassionately singing out some typical Salvation Army songs. He smiled at me like we knew each other and after giving me a knowing wink, he flashed open his ragged overcoat to show me a quart bottle of gut-rot wine nestled into one of the deep inside pockets. Later, just before bunk time, as I was outside on the front porch, he sought me out like I was his long-lost friend, asking me if I wanted to share some of his poison and then started telling me the story of his life. After the following day I flew out to Newark and forgot all about that man.

Side Note:

Oddly enough, two years later, I was back in Portland, walking from a guitar shop off Madison Street, cutting through a small city block park there when someone in front of me called out. I looked over to see Mr. Paul, sitting on a shaded park bench with two other gentlemen, passing a bottle between them. He told me that he'd just got into town and was looking for a place to crash. I gave him my address, told him to try to be there by eleven, and from Mr. Paul's expressed excitement, I expected to see him, but he never showed. After midnight, I went to sleep.

Another Side Note:

I was staying at the Kingston Apartments, a kind of, flop-house hotel for the down and out and elderly living on their Social Security checks. I was ascending the dilapidated stairwell to get to my room on the second floor when I saw a man lying drunk, halfway up the stairs. He was sprawled in a kind of fetus position over three or four stairs, with the neck of a Seagram Seven bottle precariously balanced just inside the torn-out left pocket of his shabby overcoat. A drunk on the stairs was a common sight and I just about passed over him when he made this weird sound that, frightened me. I stopped, knelt down and seeing his eyes opened, asked if he would like help getting to his room. He nodded and with one arm on my shoulder, brought him to his room.

He told me later that he was now living off a small pension that helped him pay for his room, buy cigarettes, booze and occasionally food.

Kingston Apartments - Portland Oregon

At the expense of an infrequent bummed cigarette, I spent some time listening to more of his life stories. Although there was an age difference between us and I could not fully relate to much of his uninteresting work experiences, there were many life-learned insights given from his obscure perceptions and from the esoteric wisdom within his prudent stories. I was moved by his great passion and love for his wife that he had foolishly yet regrettably left years earlier over a stupid argument about money. I perceived that by then, he had arrived to a point in his life where the values he moralized were clouded by his own inability to care about anything but where and when his next drink might be coming from. Even after he had just gotten up in the morning, (10:00), he looked horrible and had that cough that would not stop until he filled his lungs with the smoke of a filter-less Pall Mall. It was during one of these times that he told me that although I was different from him, I was only a bottle and a ditch away from being dealt the same fate in life as he had. A couple of months later, he was once again too drunk to climb up the stairs to his room and he just fell asleep halfway up the landing. It was a very cold February night when I came home about 2:00 in the morning and saw him there in a heap, balled up in his overcoat. After a hard time trying to wake him up and listening to him spew every obscenity, he could think of to be left alone,

I finally got him to respond and I helped him up the stairs. Because he was in such a drunken state, I was goofing on him and his lack of comprehension. It was a lot of fun to hear him respond to my nonsense gibberish and thinly veiled disrespectful harassments and I had a hard time just keeping from laughing as we moved down the vacant hall. Still, even in his drunken state he kept asking me to forgive him for swearing at me as we stumbled down the hallway to his room. He dropped onto his bed, still fully clothed and still wearing that overcoat with the left pocket torn out. I threw an old army blanket over him and turned out the light. As I was leaving, he said something inaudible to me and laughed. I muttered something in return to pacify him and left for my room down the hall. A couple of days later he was found dead in his bed, still fully dressed, wearing his overcoat and covered by a wool blanket. To this day I still wonder what his last words to me were.

But I Changed My Mind

(Written in 1984) – In January 1973, Richard Nixon announced an accord with North Vietnam to end American involvement in Indochina. In 1974, his Secretary of State, Henry Kissinger, negotiated disengagement agreements between Israel and its opponents, Egypt and Syria; but the war waged on in the Middle East and in Asia.

Side Note:

Nixon defeated Democratic candidate George McGovern in 1972 by a wide margin, (some say from a rigged election and tampered ballot boxes), and within a few months, his administration was embattled over the so-called "Watergate" scandal, stemming from a break-in at the offices of the Democratic National Committee during that 1972 campaign. The break-in was traced to officials of the Committee to Re-elect the President. A number of administration officials resigned; some were later convicted of offenses connected with efforts to cover up the affair. Nixon denied any personal involvement, but the courts forced him to yield tape recordings, which indicated that he had, in fact, tried to divert the investigation. As a result of unrelated scandals in Maryland, Vice President Spiro T. Agnew resigned in 1973 and was replaced by Gerald R. Ford. Faced with what seemed almost certain impeachment, Nixon announced on August 8, 1974, that he would resign the next day to begin "that process of healing which is so desperately needed in America." In his last years, Nixon gained praise as an elder statesman. By the time of his death on April 22, 1994, he had written numerous books on his experiences in public life and on foreign policy. There is a time when you have to wonder where someone else's head must be at and why they can possibly be thinking the things they do and the reasons for this odd thought. I struggled with my own distain for this man for quite some time and almost changed my opinion and my mind, almost.

Another Side Note:

I was experimenting with clichés and phrases, trying to put them into lyrics for songs. It seemed like the right thing to do because you already had this built in hook. I took the phrase, "I changed my mind" and joined it with "a change of heart," threw in motive and regret and concluded with the phrase, "you were the best thing that ever happened to me," but I couldn't make the meter work, so I changed it to, "you were the best thing I ever had," and the song was done. I don't do this song much anymore, but I don't think it would take much to dust it off and use it again.

I Been There Before

(Written in 1985) – In the late seventies and early eighties I was an unhappy person going nowhere, feeling like I'd failed Diane and the kids with my paltry financial circumstances and lack of direction. I decided to go back to school and become a draftsman. From all this stress and disappointment, I was going through, it became evident in my songwriting with everything turning out to reflect something rather depressing. After leaving JW Electronics in the spring of 1982 and after a series of different jobs, I went to work at the Forest Funeral Home. It was there that I regained a positive spin on life again. It was there that

I started to write positive, substantive songs again. This is one of those songs that kind of fit into a few genres of music but never was much more than another one of those songs.

Early Morning Sun

(Written in 1991) – In the late 70s and early 80s I was an unhappy person going nowhere. It became evident in my songwriting with everything rather depressing. I left J. W. Electronics in 1982 and after a series of different jobs went to work at Forest Funeral Home. It was there that I regained a positive spin on life again. It was there that I started to write positive, independent songs again. This is one of those.

Dream Your Troubles To Sleep

(Written in 1973) – Somewhere between the time when I had my first child Loren, and us moving to the Chinese Castle on the other side of Portland, I wrote this song, mostly for Lori but also for all my children afterwards. How appropriate this song would have been if I would have written this after I had some experience with children and with bedtimes. What I came to find out was that raising children wasn't quite as ideological as a song portrays. A lullaby for little people's slumber. Perhaps an idealistic lullaby from an impractical mental picture of a quiet, restful evening after putting the kids to bed.

Side Note:

This song has a lot of intrinsic truths within the confines of the lyrics. Every one of my children since has enjoyed me playing this song for them, perhaps not realizing that in fact, I was trying to get them to go to sleep so that I could go on with the rest of my evening life.

Crazy Cars

(Written in 1972) – In 1972 there was no gasoline crisis and in fact the term MPG had not even been a defining consideration to the public. My main mode of transportation at the time was a bicycle, which I pedaled all over the city of Portland. But in my travels one of the things I noticed was this huge transportation problem, especially downtown, which only seem to get worse every time I tried to shortcut my way to the Kingston Apartments by going down one-way streets the wrong way. Meanwhile, in October 1973, there was an oil crisis when members of the Organization of Arab Petroleum Exporting Countries, proclaimed an oil embargo. The embargo was targeted at nations perceived as supporting Israel during the Yom Kippur War. Canada, Japan, the Netherlands, the United Kingdom and the United States were the initial nations targeted, with the embargo also later extended to Portugal, Rhodesia and South Africa. By the end of the embargo in March 1974, the price of oil had risen nearly 300%, from 3 dollars per barrel to nearly $12 globally; US prices were significantly higher. A month later, in April of 1974, I went down to a local radio station in southeast Portland, (KBOO) and playing this song. The two DJs were impressed by the song, but one of them was impressed by my insight to the oil crisis, feeling the song was rather apocalyptic and had a doomsday feel to it.

Side Note:

To this day I wonder why it took the American Motors Companies, like Chrysler, or Ford, General Motors, so many years after the influx of the Japanese imports to realize the boat car was done. More than anyone else, the American car industry was guilty for that second Japanese invasion—the compact car. Maybe it was the oil companies press, wanting to drink in the profits of the gas guzzler, maybe they were so used to cutting corners, or maybe they were so in love with their own products that they were blind to what the other guy; their customer wanted, either way or neither way, it would be almost ten years later before they would actually do something about the problem and come out weakly with a competing small car and would be at least five more years after that before they came out with a notable product that was competition for the Japanese vehicles made by Honda and Toyota. Arguably, from obvious resale values and longevity products, and it saddens me that the American car industry never did step up to make their cars compete with the same quality of the Japanese imports, but I still believe they could.

Forget-Me-Nots

(Written in 1990) – While working at the funeral home, I supervised or officiated at many of the funeral and memorial services. This left me many opportunities to bring leftover fresh flowers and potted plants home to Diane. There was this one service where the family was overwhelmed with flowering plants and cut flowers, so afterwards, they divided everything up and then insisted that I bring home a collection of the flowers and potted plants to my wife Diane. I ended up with this tiny arrangement of forget-me-nots and was intrigued by their tiny beauty. Each collection of pedals of each tiny face of each flower is unique and yet together shines a wonderful color. I drew a correlation between that plant and each tiny deed of each little unique moment that is special, and yet together these deeds and acts of kindness shines a wonderful thing called love. I wrote some of these lyrics down that day on a small piece of paper and promptly lost it for about 5 years. The plant lived for a while and went the way of all plants to the fate of a gardeneress with a non-green thumb, but the song lived on.

How Does One

(Written in 1982) – After I got fired from JW electronics, I went to work for a large construction Company in Jacksonville Florida, called Burns and Roe, where I did drafting or to be more specific I did revisions of other people's drafting. Unfortunately, the promises that were made and what truly happened were at such great odds that I had no choice but to leave Jacksonville and come back to Olympia Washington. Although I had a small house payment and we were able to take advantage of welfare offered by the LDS Church, for the next couple of months, things were kind of hard. I felt that I had become rather downhearted and difficult to get along with. I'm sure that Diane had her hands full, dealing with four little kids and me. Anyway, one night, feeling sorry for myself, I wrote this song. Looking back at this song, this time period and what was going on all around me, it still kind of hurts. But I loved the tune that went with the lyrics, and I kept all of it in my head for years until I was able to document it.

All The Man I Was

(Written in 1985) – In the funeral business there is a certain service called pre-need which offered to people that are still living, a prearrangement of their funeral matters. There was this small Asian-American man with an incurable disease that came in with his wife and made arrangements with me to have everything paid for in advance. He wanted to make sure his wife would not have to do or pay anything at the time of his death. I was impressed by the way he handled himself and his wife in this undoubtedly difficult time. After handling the pre-need funeral arrangements, I sat at the funeral home's newly acquired programmable Corona typewriter and composed the lyrics to this song. On a different note, during the time I was there at the funeral home, this Asian-American man never did pass away, but he would call me up every few months and ask, "Is everything still all right?"

Side Note:

Honor and responsibility to one's self and family and realizing that a person's name and reputation are linked to the respect a person gains from others. This then ties in with that person's perceived personal worth and sense of conduct wherein lies the integrity of all the man he might be.

Down The Road

(Written in 1979) – In 1979, after working for JW electronics for five years, I was disillusioned and disappointed with my own direction and career. Even though my father-in-law owned the company, his perception of me was less than sterling as I found myself being passed over from one promotion to another. One day I walked into the office and told my father-in-law that I quit and I went to work for a cardboard factory, run by a large company called Georgia Pacific. I was in fact, a pilot: that is to say, I picked things up and I piled it here and I picked things up and I piled it there and that was my existence in my job for three months. We were going through the Carter Administration recession; times were hard and I was laid off. I was working for Ray down in Oregon, and while I was carrying a box of nails into an unlit repair shop, I fell five feet down into one of those grease-monkey pits, you know, where they drive a car over the hole in the concrete to work on the motor, anyway, I ended up braking my leg and I was in a cast for about two months. Being unhappy or contemplative with who and where I was in my life and contemplating my planned/unplanned career. Because I was off work for a while, I decided to go back to school. It wasn't too long after that, that Georgia-Pacific wanted me to go back to work for them. The long and short of the whole story is, I ended up back at JW Electronics for about another three years before I was fired by my brother-in-law. It was during this time that I wrote the song "Down The Road," to reflect my unhappiness and uncertainty with that job and also with my life. I couldn't take comfort in the fact that I was wealthy beyond comprehension with my wonderful, loving wife and family. Anyway, I wrote this song to denote the line, "When a man decides it must be time to go, even while he's working, he's halfway down the road."

Prairie Moon

(Written in 1949) – Almost everything in my collection of songs are exclusively written by, composed by, and sung by that guy, Lord Baldwin; but this song was the first exception. One day I was down on the farm in Aurora Oregon, cleaning out animal stalls, while my dad watched. I was talking about some of the songs I had been recording at this time and some of the songs that I had written. He told me in a "matter of fact" tone that he had written some songs himself. I was intrigued. I knew my father was an entertainer from way back, including burlesque and small off-Broadway-like plays, but it never occurred to me that my own father was a songwriter. I listened to a couple of his songs, and I was amazed. His most memorable or impressive song to me was this song, "Prairie Moon." I wrote down the words on the back of an envelope while he was singing the song for the umpteenth time, and memorized all the chord progressions. Afterwards, while recording the song, I took some liberties and added some supertonic and sub-median chords in place of some of my dad's proposed dominant and subdominant chords. These changes gave this song the kind of lonesome, cowboy feel that I captured when I recorded the tune.

Side Note:

I went on a campout with some Boy Scouts and some old-timer leaders and I played this song that night by the campfire. An old friend, Daniel Devoe, thought for sure that he had heard this tune. Then he thought he had heard the song before, some time in the fifties. I reassured him that it was my father who had written the song and I played it for him again. He was very impressed with the tune and thought it would be neat to get together with my dad on accordion and him on guitar to do this song, but that never happened because my father did not like driving this long distance from Aurora Oregon to Olympia Washington.

Another Side Note:

When I played my father's song to my father with the embellished chords, he really liked it and he cried, and I almost cried when I saw how much he liked me playing his material. This same thing was paralleled years later when my son Stephen started using my material in his band.

Third Side Note:

It is official, and the reason, "*Prairie Moon,*" was not included in this book of my poetry is that my father was mistaken when he claimed to have written this song. Four years after I recorded this album the internet came out, and with it, answers. It saddens me to report that this song, properly labeled, "*Roll Along Prairie Moon*," was written by, Ted Fio Rito, Albert Von Tilzer and Harry MacPherson and the song was first recorded by Ted Fio Rito, and then later by, Al Bowlly. Both had commercial recording successes in 1935.

It broke my heart to find this out, but I'm sure that my dad truly thought he had written the song and ultimately, I never confronted him on the issue. I'm sure that Ted, Albert and Harry would agree, it's better this way.

Other Notes:

-FOR YOUR INFORMATION -

I had always wanted to see what my material would sound like with other instruments like percussion, (drums), and guitars, keyboard sounds, harmonicas, all mixed down to a stereo package. Prior to recording the album, "It wasn't My Fault," I had frequented our local music store, Music 6000 and over time, played on every one of the keyboards that they had there, testing out their features and specs, all the time thinking what I could do to improve my recordings.

Unfortunately, the instruments they sold there were professional quality instruments that were way too expensive for me. I mean, a thousand dollars to me at a time when we were struggling to get by, even though I was working for the Wash. State Parks Department, those keyboards were way beyond my reach.

That is until Cousin Martha let me borrow their kid's toy Casio keyboard. It had a bank of tones, a bank of percussion beats and best of all, it had a sustain petal. It was funky, it had 80s voices and it was fun. I no longer had to take my daughter's boombox to the Lacey Stake Center, (LDS Church) to record piano bites or songs while the young men and young women were playing volleyball or basketball, in the next room, on the other side of those accordion doors. Arguably the drums had an element of cheese to them, as did some of the piano and organ tones, but for me it was now a time for me to experiment and find out what my some of my material might sound like with an accompaniment.

This album, "It wasn't My Fault," to me is like Dylan's "Bringing It All Back Home," (known as Subterranean Homesick Blues in some European countries), in many ways. This was Dylan's first album with a fusion of rock and folk music and "It wasn't My Fault," was my first album with a fusion of rock and folk music. "It wasn't My Fault," was my fifth album and "Bringing It All Back Home," was Dylan's fifth album. Now there are some other vague similarities, but Dylan's writing was and is still so far up and away and superior to my writings.

Casio CTK520L

Side Note:

This toy keyboard opened up a new awareness to what my music could be. And knowing I was to borrow the keyboard for a short time, I got really busy in the next few months, using the Casio keyboard, I recorded the, "It wasn't My Fault" album, the, "On The Open Range" album, the, "Taking Me For A Ride" album, the, "Ever On" album and a few of the songs on the, "Spinning My Wheels" album. Yes it was not perfect and arguably clunky, but it was cool to me.

81

⁂

06 - ON THE OPEN RANGE
- 1992

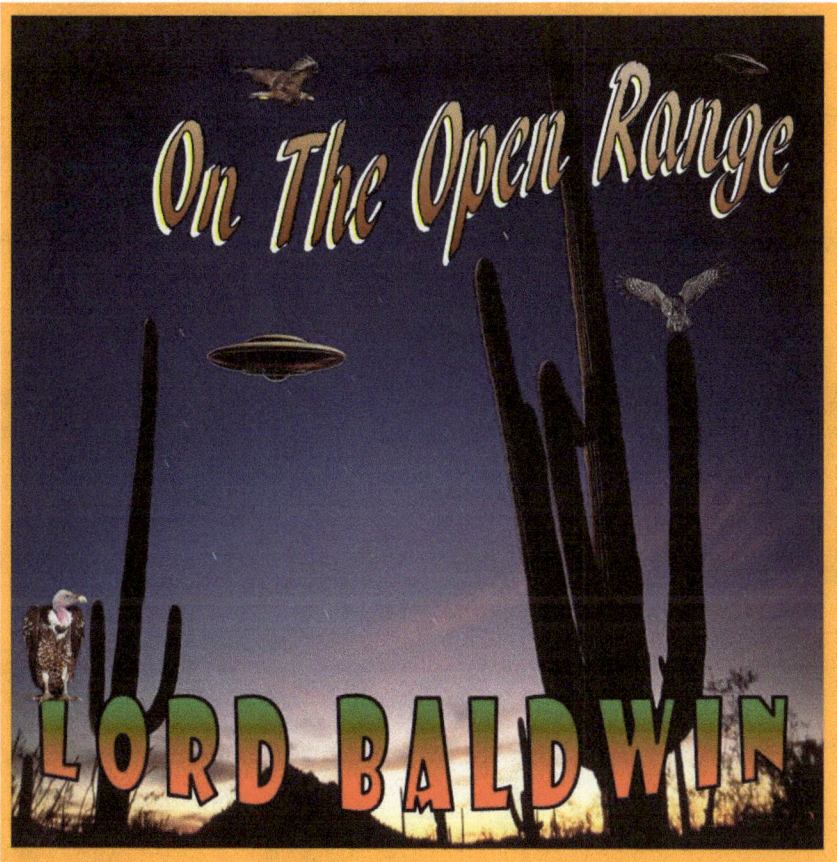

82

NOTES ABOUT THE COVERS

The original cover for, 'On The Open Range,' was another one of Salvador Dali's paintings called, 'Three Women With Heads Of Flowers Finding The Skin Of A Grand Piano On The Beach,' (1936)

It was my choice for the original art because of the spaciousness and minimal background like on a desert; but there was also the hint of music with the melted piano skin that seemed awesome, but also the painting reminded me of a scene in a Ray Bradbury story, The Martian Chronicles. (Seen below).

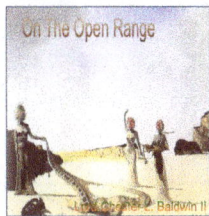

Again, the conversion from early 90s WordPerfect to 2001 MS Word lost the font

definitions, but that was okay, I had to start over from scratch anyway.

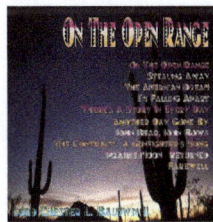

I knew there was no chance that I would be able to use that painting, so I found this desert scene where dawn was breaking, and then embellished the picture with objects like a night hawk, a desert owl and a buzzard, not to mention two or three flying saucers. I used a western type script font for the title and then added, (what I felt might be) a kind of Arizona color scheme with the Showcase Gothic font for the Lord Baldwin letters. To me, the total package and overall effect turned out great.

83

ON THE OPEN RANGE

On The Open Range
Stealing Away Again
The American Dream
I'm Falling Apart
There's A Story In Every Day
Another Day Gone By
John Bear, John Bows
The Contract (A Gunfighter's Song)
Farewell

84

On The Open Range

Well, you hunt down your food at the break of day.
and you live out of your water hole and rain.
You've lasted these five years so you think you might stay,
out here on the open range, on the open range.

There are places in some cities you could be,
ah, but here in all directions you can see.
And you know that the circle is still free,
here on the open range, on the open range.

Night falls; coyote calls,
don't you feel akin, you being all alone like him?

And of this prairie; no one is at hand,
but there's beauty in the sky and a sea of sand.
You'll probably die out on your land.
You'd like all the people to change,
ah, but you're here all alone and you sure feel strange.
but a hermit; you're bound to remain,
here on the open range, on the open range.

85

Stealing Away Again

Well, I'm a worker of an endless day,
and though I work hard, I don't get much pay,
and it's only enough to buy records now and then,
to be stealing away.

I don't get breaks and I make mistakes,
but never twice that way, I get better everyday,
and they say I'm going higher but they never say when
so, I'm stealing away, stealing away again.

Oh, stealing away again,
can't say when I'll be back cause I don't know when.
And I'm feeling that the minds of men
are stealing away,... stealing away again.

I've heard of folks who got their freedom of mind,
I'd like to know where they find all that time
cause I'm tired all the time and night is the only time
when I can be stealing away.

I've got a thought and I've got a voice,
I'm even told daily that I've got a choice,
and I know I've got a dream of the true and the fair,
someday I'm going to wake up and find myself there

just stealing away again,
can't say when I'll be back cause I don't know when.
And I'm feeling that the minds of men
are stealing away,... stealing away again.

Stealing away again,
back through the pasture and down in the glen.
And I'm knowing that the truth is then
just stealing away, stealing away again.

86

The American Dream

I chased the good life; forgot about the bad times.
I didn't think that it could fall down on me.
I ran with fast crowds; forsaking my true friends.
Without consequences, I thought I should always be free.
I had some good friends; leastwise I thought them to be.
When my money flowed
those good comrades were always around.
I knew another side, people that cared for me.
But I didn't want them worrying
where I could be found.

But why did I have to waste my life?
Now I'm called to pay this price.
Even now I wonder as it all falls down on me,
I was a fool to pursue and never reach the American dream.

Time was no tool of mine; I had no goals or plans.
I'd run with the pack, and I was reckless and wild.
But soon it fell apart, so scared watching from the stands,
I ran from reality just like a little child.

And why did I have to waste my life?
Now I'm called to pay this price.
Even now I wonder as it all falls down on me,
I was a fool to pursue and never reach
the American dream.

The American dream, to strive and succeed.
A fine house, new car and two point five kids.
But I stepped on everything to achieve my own needs,
still the loss was mine in the final end. T
he loss was all mine in the final end.

I chased the good life, forgot about the bad times.
I didn't think that it could ever fall down on me.
Too late for sorrys now, bridges are long past burned.
It's such a shame to look back and know what should be.

And why did I have to waste my life?
For now I'm called to pay the price.
Even now I wonder as it all falls down on me,
I was a fool to pursuit and never reach,...
How could I have let it all get by my life?
. I was a fool to pursue and never reach
the American dream.

87

I'm Falling Apart

You were right when you said that I would regret
my decision to leave you back then.
It hit me some date but I found it too late
to change things over again.
I tried to turn things around but too late; I have found
that I just didn't know where to start.
So, I'm singing these blues; wondering what I should do,
and it's funny, but I'm falling apart.

In a memory lapse, I might start to collapse
hey, and forget where or why I am here.
I could be at a ball game; someone mentions your name,
and I can't speak, with my eyes fill with tears.
I ain't doing so well and I have heard tell
this is brought on by a broken heart.
Although I might try, I still can't deny
that it's funny and I'm falling apart.

I could use help in the mornings,
when things just don't work out right.

I need a little help in the evenings,
when it's so hard to cope with the night.

You were right when you said that I would regret
my decision to leave you alone.
Though I play this role, I am out of control
and my heart has a mind of its own.
it calls out to you and I know it's true
to forgive and forget is an art.
Still I'm singing these blues, wondering what I should do,
and it's funny, I'm falling apart.
Funny, I'm falling apart.

88

There's A Story In Every Day

He'd been trying to get work but to make matters worse,
his doctor last week said he had a cancer curse.
Glen gathered his family and together in prayer
asked the Lord to take care of his family there.
Resigned to his fate, he still reached out to everyone,
and he finds with each new morning, that his life is far from done.
With thanks to the Lord, the family knelt to pray,
there's a story in every day.

There's a story in every day, and a part that we're all bound to play.
From the moment we're born, till we're carried away,
there's a story in every day.

On Tuesday, Jill's husband ran off from their home.
He took all the money and left her and four kids alone.
She blamed herself for not being the sweet perfect wife,
that might have kept him at home
and might have even made better; their life.
She couldn't find work, and everything seemed to go wrong,
but her family all pitched in and helped her along.

And as time passes, she found a strength and a side she can play;
and there's a story in every day.

There's a story in every day,
and a morning that we're all bound to play.
From the moment we're born till we're carried away,
there's a story in every day.

On Friday, the bank came to visit Uncle Joe.
As Joe opened the door he smiled and said, "I know".
"But with Sarah sick in bed, and my mill job up and quit,
I had to kind of let the little things slide just a bit".
The bank man interrupted, wouldn't even let him get through—
and he said, "I'm Sorry, Sir, but I got my job to do."
With a hope for tomorrow, Joe and his family drove away,
and there's a story in every day.

There's a story in every day, and a roll that we're all bound to play.
From the moment we're born, till we're carried away,
there's a story in every day.

And we all have a choice each day as we wake,
how we're going to approach all we do and all that we say.
And we can see all the bad and be bitter of life,
or we can look for the moments that make living so nice.
How we act, and react to that world in our sight,
makes the life that we live, important or trite.
No matter how we approach things you know,
they'll arrive anyway,
and that there's a story in every day.

There's a story in every day, and a roll that we're all bound to play.
From the moment we're born, till we're carried away,
there's a story in every day,... there's a story in every day.

89

Another Day Gone By

With all the technology rushing forward,...
progress driving upwards all the time.
Discoveries and advancements that shape the world,
nice to know we're not falling behind.
Still, people are starving and dying,
while others have forgotten how to cry.
Secure in our shell, if we don't look, we can't tell,
it just becomes another day gone by.

Another day gone by; another day gone by,
Secure in our shell, if we don't look, we can't tell,
it just becomes another day gone by.

As the political façade entraps us,
and discourses of nothing are expressed,
one wonders the furtive ambitions and goals that hide
behind the ends being blessed.
Still, people in desperate trouble, feel betrayed and ask, "Why try"?
Don't play any role for they'll always have control
it just becomes another day gone by.

Another day gone by; another day gone by,
Don't play any role for they'll always have control
it just becomes another day gone by.

When a long-worked person retires,
the long-awaited rest seems deserved.
Looking over the fleeting years gone by, with all,;
there was a pleasure to have served.
Still, people need some confirmation
there's something to show for their life,
for if they lose who they are or what they've done so far,
it just becomes another day gone by.

Another day gone by; another day gone by,
If they lose who they are or what they've done so far,
it just becomes another day gone by.

From the depths of despair and sorrow,
to the joy that the truth has brought.
Rewards and fine stations in lifetimes
seem trite to eternal goals sought.
Still, people need some reassurance
that their hopes weren't really a lie.
Without faith and a hope, life is meaningless and cold
and just becomes another day gone by.

Another day gone by; another day gone by,
Without faith and a hope, life is meaningless and cold
and just becomes another day gone by.

90

John Bear, John Bows

He was born of good parents; he was raised in loving hands.
He never sought to do evil or take the life of another man.
Even when a mob came and burned his home
and took all his family had,
John stood behind the wisdom and the strength of his humble dad.
John Bear, John Bows.

John never wished to run from what the just arm of the law said,
but in a dream, he was warned that there was danger just ahead.
So, he packed what he could carry and he lit out in the dark,
leaving all his life behind him with a bounty unjustly marked.
It was early in the morning; they came to take him in.
the crime would be for something that he never really did.
With shotguns they busted down the doors
to take him dead or alive
but though they moved in quickly, nobody could ever find,
John Bear, John Bows.

Many men tried to bring him in for a profit or a name,
but john was quick and foxlike leaving them all on a wild chase.

Just when the thought they had him
penned up just beyond the bend,
John would cover his tracks,
leaving them again down some dead end.
From the ridges of Kentucky to the hills of Tennessee,
all through this endless hunting, nobody could ever reach
John Bear, John Bows.

A story came from Wyoming where winter had set in.
A plot was schemed by four bad and desperate men.
While one challenged John out in the streets
three hid behind some doors
but after shots rang out and the smoke cleared,
all but John lay dead on the floor.
Some thought he died thereafter
from the damage the bad had done
still others thought they seen him on his way to Oregon.
John Bear, John Bows.

Now many say old John is dead but most, well just don't know.
Some seen him in Alaska, others swear he's in New Mexico.
One thing they all agree on, that he was a goodly man,
only out to keep himself alive in a country with other plans.
Some people knew him as John Bear, others as John Bows,
fact is, his name and whereabouts, most folks will never know.
John Bear, John Bows.

91

The Contract (A Gunfighter's Song)

Darkness at noon, last night a black moon,
seems the times are telling me what is gonna be soon.

Ah, you fool, you think to make a name, you'll win my hand or die
take this title off my gun belt and wear it in your eye.
I can tell you where it's at, riding high in the saddle and free,
still always looking back to see
if someone is coming after me.

I'm the fastest in these parts, been that way since sixty-one.
I've slapped leather with the best around, and every time I won.
Only, time has caused me casualties and I'm shaky when I stand,
and my two-gun style is haunted
by arthritis in my right hand.

Ah, but you hear not a thing, an icy stare you cast so cool.
Your determination blinds your eyes and binds you to this duel.
Lightning speed, a steady hand, will hold this hour's day,

but this albatross you wager for
can only leave one to walk away.

Right now, walk away,
before I blow you down.
WALK AWAY!!

Oh, the funeral was so quiet, just some families and friends
I could see them all looking over at me; wondering when I'll end.
I pack my bags, get out of town; I'm riding fast and long,
yet, I wonder just how long it'll be
before I fall into something wrong.

Right now, walk away,
before I blow you down.
Please, WALK AWAY!!

9²

Farewell

And to those who have a road ahead
and them with payment past due.
For them who'll be lost tomorrow,
and those just passing through.
To all with good intentions
that carry us to this day,
with sights and hopes for peace and love
in a world that's slipping away.
Oh, I bid thee farewell.
Farewell; I bid the farewell.
And to all the unknown heroes
that revel in righting the wrong.
For them who side with the underdog,
for the cause well spent along.
To all who carry those banners high
with full knowledge of what might come to be,
yet stand unmoved courageously
as the world comes apart at the seams,
I bid thee farewell.
Farewell, Farewell; I bid the farewell.

93

⸙

MEMOIRS & NOTES -06 -
'ON THE OPEN RANGE'

On The Open Range

(Written 1973) – Although this poem was written in 1973, it was from a memory that I had had three years earlier. After a long time of being unemployed in Oregon, I decided that I would travel east through Canada and then back down to the Catskills to work as a waiter at Passover. I had sown an American flag on the right side of my backpack, to be seen as I was hitchhiking, for curious Canadians to see and maybe want to give a ride to talk to an American. Unfortunately, I got stuck in Saskatchewan and I spent three days about a few miles east of Medicine Hat with no rides before I realized I was running out of time and so I came back into the states.

At the border one of the patrol men stepped over and violently ripped off my American flag and punched me in the gut with it, motioning with a nod for me to take it.

It was the middle of the Vietnam era where a lot of kids my age were going across the border into Canada to avoid the draft. The two border patrolmen questioned me for over an hour, trying, I think, to see if I would change my story if told at another time. After punishing me for that long while I was let back into the United States, close to dusk, hampering with my limited timeframe.

While hitchhiking the 250 miles, I got a ride that took me all the way down highway 87 into Billings Montana; the state with the big blue-sky country.

It was on that long stretch of prairie road that I remember looking out the window of the car, maybe doing 70 miles an hour and seeing this little shack about a half mile off, and I saw what appeared to be this old man standing by some other structure, presumably a well, and he looked like he was cleaning a rabbit or some other small animal carcass.

There was, in the back of the house, an outhouse and curiously, there were no electrical poles or wires running over to his small cabin. Imagining that there was no plumbing or electricity, I thought to myself that his existence, out in that forsaken desert place, was very primitive or at least back to early-American basics.

This person and his shack out in the middle of nowhere moved me, and although dormant in my mind for a few years, the thought of that lifestyle inspired me. And from my observations, of his out-in-the-middle-of-nowhere isolationism and my thoughts of his dealing with the lonely life of a recluse, which, going as fast as the car was traveling, could have only lasted in a matter of a few minutes, still, from that brief encounter, the essence of the song was imbedded in my mind for retrieval later on.

Side Note:

Years later, I had this dream that I was with the family coming back home from a trip to Disneyland, when our white, 1965 Plymouth Fury III station wagon broke down in a small town out in the middle of nowhere. We had the car towed to a small garage where they were working on replacing the radiator hoses and replacing the water pump.

There I was with Diane and four small kids sitting on a bench sweltering in the shade of the awning just outside the shop when a song came on the radio. It was this song, "On The Open Range," but it was being covered by a group called "America."

"That's my song." I yelled coming in close to where the radio was perched or mounted up above the doorway leading into the office area. To this day, I can still remember how hopeless I felt standing there listening to some other group doing my song.

Another Side Note:

From a different perspective, and even though it was a dream, hearing this song performed with a country-like three-part harmony was actually very awesome.

Stealing Away Again

(Written 1972) – In my early years of guitar mastery, I experimented with a lot of different chord progressions, most especially, getting away from the basic tonic, sub-dominant. Tonic, dominant, tonic progression.

In 1972 my assets and possessions consisted of a change of clothing, a few harmonicas, my guitar, a record player, a cool pair of brown Beatle boots, and a small but powerful collection of records. At the time that I wrote this poem, I had left Burger Chef and was self-employed. To get by, I was working construction, mostly concrete flatwork, along with assorted exterior house painting jobs.

Side Note:

The words of this poem reflect that moment when I was back home, I'm done working, and all I want is to just kickback, relax, play some music, and let everything else go away. Although I was staying at the Kingston Apartment, which in many circles could be considered a flop house, I kind of felt that I was inside, breaking out or away from the constructs of the working-man's day, and tuned in with the minds of men, who were all stealing away again.

The American Dream

(Written 1982) – This was one of the first poems that I wrote after I got past the post depression of leaving, (being fired), from JW

Electronics. At the funeral home, in a different mindset, I reflected on my pursuits of the American dream or at least what I perceived to be the American dream. I was toying around with some chords on the piano when this tune came out. It all pretty much evolved from part of the chorus that said, "why did I have to waste my life, for now I'm called to pay the price. Even now I wonder as it all falls down on me, I was a fool to pursue and never reach; the American dream."

Side Note:

In truth, I wrote the lyrics kind of from the perspective of some-body that really had wasted his time and talents on frivolous and fleeting cheap thrills. But most of the little esoteric lines had a basis of truth and personal experience to them. A person in search of the American dream while realizing that he has wasted most of his life in idle play. Perhaps my perspective was warped, but to this day, I have never reached or truly achieved what I believed then to be the essence of what the American dream truly was.

I'm Falling Apart

(Written 1991) – This poem was written in late 1991 after I heard a neat little song on the radio by Merle Haggard. I was so impressed that I wrote the words to what I remembered of that tune. Not more than a week later, I was dinking around with some other chords and came up with this version of what the tune is now. Maybe not surprisingly, after I put the new tune and the revised words together and came up with this song, "I'm falling apart," I forgot all about how the other tune went.

Side Note:

After I finished writing the words and put a tune to it, I was playing it for a friend of mine who thought he might record it. This was a flattering thought, but I really wasn't ready to have some other person, who was also an unknown in the music industry, kick around and maybe lose one my songs. And so it went, I recorded the song and then prophetically, it pretty much became forgotten. Years later I searched for that song of Merle Haggard's, but to this day, I've never found it, but if you're out there reading this note, thank you Merle for the inspiration.

There's A Story In Every Day

(Written 1991) – Originally when I wrote this poem, my idea was to have a Texas-speaking monologue that portrayed different people's trials, with the hopeful realization that if you look close enough, there is a serious drama going on in everyone's life. Then the chorus would be sung by me, saying, "there's a story in every day, and a part we are all bound to play. From the moment were born till we're carried away, there's a story in every day."

Unfortunately, sometimes reality never comes across what you had envisioned in your mind, and the end result for me was this off-point but acceptable substitute. I may take another run at this another time.

Side Note:

I was never in love with this song. I mean, maybe if I recorded it differently and embellished it with,... I don't know, it wasn't one of my go-to songs. But meanwhile, my friend George Dillabough commented after reviewing the album that this one particular song was one of his favorite songs that I'd ever written. This completely surprised me, because I thought he had better taste in music than that.

Another Day Gone By

(Written 1984) – When I wrote the words to this poem I feel like I had come into my own style of songwriting. Philosophical thoughts hounded the foundation of my own beliefs, I was confused by the bourgeoisie-kind of thinking that has been going on for hundreds of years. Like so many others that stare up into the star-lit night pondering their existence, I found myself questioning the meaning of life. The words of the end of this poem, "without faith and hope, life is meaningless and cold" was a paramount thought throughout the whole poem. I changed the tune, which originally had a lot of minor and sad musical phrases, to reflect a sense of positive energy.

Side Note:

I stopped amplifying negative perspectives of life that typified the concept of just another dreary day gone by; and I livened it up a little bit, added a chorus that repeated and reiterated the last lines of the stanzas. This newer tune, like many songs from that era that needed a keyboard to carry the mood, was complimented with the sound of that old organ in the funeral Chapel. The message I was striving for was a study on how we perceive our lives and what goes on around us from the comparison versus the reality of half-empty perspectives.

John Bear, John Bows

(Written 1978) – Because I am a member of the Church of Jesus Christ of Latter-Day Saints, many of my compadres, after hearing this song, believed that I was parodying the life and times of Joseph Smith Jr., but this is not the case. If anyone, I would say that Porter Rockwell could have played a part, Jeremiah Johnson, maybe, but as mentioned before and may again be mentioned later, many of my songs are inspirations or documentations of ideas, thoughts, and even musical tunes collected from my dreams. John Bear is one of those songs that came to me in a dream, and it kind of played out like in a movie.

In the dream, I was this John Bear who, lost everything; all of his possessions, as well as his reputation and the life that he knew, from his personal and or religious convictions. An odd thing in this particular dream was that, like Nat King Cole in Cat Ballou, I was also a traveling minstrel documenting the life and times of this wilderness man named, John Bear as the cinematography and story-line continued. Except for a few ideas that I embellished; my dream embodied most of the main ideas that became documented into the poem.

Side Note:

The kind-of whooping, yodel-like sounds I make in the chorus were founded one night in my daughter Liz's room when she was about 8 months old. She woke up one evening, upset that she was alone and in her crib. I came in with my guitar, still working on the song and as I got to the chorus, I did that "John Bows—who hoo hoo hoo" thing which surprised and must have delighted her, because she stopped crying immediately. It was a trick that I used for years and many babies since. Because of the fast-paced tempo, this song quickly became a favorite of all the kids, and I myself, played it nightly upon request.

The Contract (The Gunfighter's Song)

(Written 1972) – It's pretty obvious that this song was developed from the old-West type theme with a stereotypical gunfighter that rides into a town, weary from his journey, only to be confronted by someone younger than him; perhaps even a kid, whose only desire is to take the gunfighter's name and reputation away. My thought was to try to add some human frailty to the gunfighter himself, like getting older and having human frailties like arthritis, and to get into the mindset of this gunfighter, that, for whatever reason, only wants to put away his guns and live the rest of his life somewhere in peace. Unfortunately, he finds his reputation proceeds him wherever he goes and he ends up always needing to defend himself and his ill-gotten reputation or lose his own life.

Prairie Moon

(Written 1949) – (See Prairie Moon, No. 1, "It Wasn't My Fault.") As mentioned before, when I recorded this song, I thought it was written by my father, and, because I usually record two 45-minute albums at one time, and put them both on one 90 min. tape. I spaced out thinking that I was revisiting "Prairie Moon" in the album, "It Wasn't My Fault," which was on the other side of this tape. Well, never mind the fact that one version was recorded at regular speed, and the other was recorded at very low speed. When I came back to this song, the second version, I took the very low speed and sped up really fast, then added my voice over the chipmunk voice that was already there. This gave the song a different feel and tempo that I couldn't help including in this album.

Side Note:

Coming from a new sense of now, after finding out that my dad was mistaken when he believed, and told me, that he had written this song, obviously for copyright purposes, seeing as how, "Roll Along Prairie Moon," was written by, Ted Fio Rito, Albert Von Tilzer and Harry MacPherson, (in 1935), I could not include either version when I published and distributed "On The Open Range," or, "It Wasn't My Fault." As mentioned before, four years after I recorded this album the internet came out, and with a little research I found out the reality of things.

Another Side Note:

I still haven't told my dad the truth, I think I like the idea of him continuing to reminisce and remember that "Prairie Moon," was, and is, his song.

Farewell

(Written 1970) – This was one of my early songs that I wrote while still trying to learn how to play the piano and sing at the same time. Prior to me going back to the Catskills to work as a waiter at Passover, I spent some time trying to find work somewhere, anywhere in the Portland area. The song is about a traveler so to speak, perhaps myself, who, on his many journeys and paths that he follows down, finds another traveler who is searching for his/her own meaning in life, like themselves/myself. Perhaps as the traveler, I speak to all who not only know about the golden rule but lives by it, and I bid them Farewell as I would have others do me the same good Farewell. I don't know if it was the way I looked, my apparent attitude or the way I presented myself, but that winter of 1970 **Side Note:**

was really non productive, except for my short stint working 13 hours a day at the chicken farm, shoveling chicken manure. (Oh yeah, like working on a chicken farm can be considered constructive and rewarding), yet I spent the majority of most of my mornings searching for work, on the eastside or walking the pavements in downtown Portland, or Beaverton, or Hillsborough with little to no success. By the afternoon I was usually disappointed and depressed and usually found myself at Portland State University in one of the piano rooms practicing and composing musical works. This song was composed there and was in the, part-two phase, so to speak, of my piano playing style. I was experimenting and trying to change my tempo and timing to accommodate this song and what I wanted to do with it.

94

07 - TAKING ME FOR A
RIDE - 1992

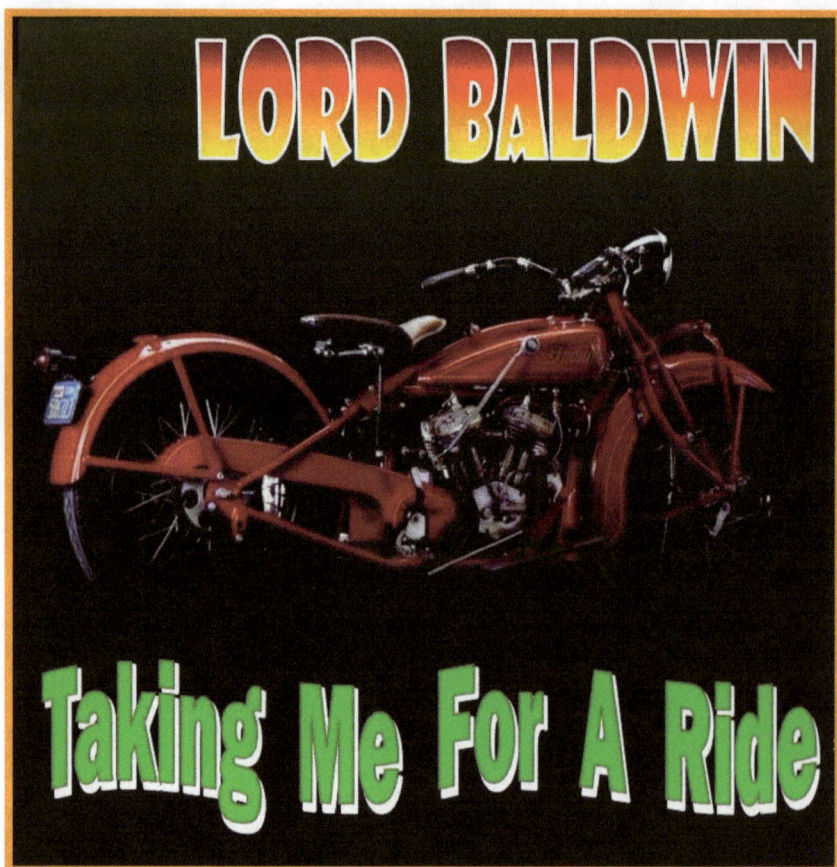

95

NOTES ABOUT THE
COVERS

This is pretty much the same cover I used in 1992. (See below). It was so great, to have this Indian motorcycle for the cover for a few reasons, first, because the now, infamous song, The Ballad Of Hank Skelly, was on this album, mostly about the life and times of Hank Skelly, a real cool head, with his 54 Duo-Glide, Harley Davidson, but I think he'd appreciate the nod to this American Indian motorcycle, and also, when I was 14, one of my friend's, dad restored a WWII 841 Indian motorcycle and painted it Candy Apple Red. It had a drive shaft instead of a chain belt (and Rory's dad let me drive it). And even though it was only for a few blocks, I really dug its sound and its feel. It was awesome!

Below are the original front and back covers.

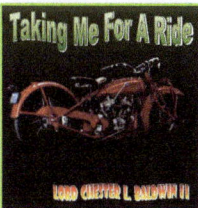

96

TAKING ME FOR A RIDE

Taking Me For A Ride
Ballad Of Hank Skelly
Cruising While I'm Losing
Shoes Are For The Domesticated Feet
Running Away
The Mud Puddle
One Day At A Time
Just Another Bimmy (Number 1)
Don't Make Me Beg For Your Love

97

Taking Me For A Ride

"Say young man, you're doing great, we've got lots of plans for you.
The sky's the limit with your potential,
you'll be on top before you're through."
The words pour out of his mouth so smooth
I'd plan for the raise ahead,
but I been down that road before,
ain't much truth to what he's said.

They're taking me for a ride. Playing my faith with words that lie.
Can't see much while I'm starry-eyed, they're taking me for a ride.
"Hey, tall, dark and handsome, what are you doing after nine?
Why don't we hit the hot spots
and have ourselves a real good time."
She comes on like a freight train,
with the tempting plans she's made,
but I know where the bills go when the piper wants to be paid.

She's taking me for a ride. Playing my emotions against my pride.
I've lost my better judgment inside, she's taking me for a ride.
"Get your education paid for, you'll have a chance to see the world.

Room and board, completely paid for
and with every port, a different girl."
It sounds too good to be true, so I'm taken in and carried away.
But reality doesn't hit until it's too late
as I'm on a scow in San Diego Bay.

They're taking me for a ride.
I don't know what hit me from behind.
Too late, with nowhere left to hide,
they're taking me for a ride.

98

The Ballad Of Hank Skelly

A hundred and thirteen pounds, five foot one,
boots and leathers, he didn't scare up none.
But looks can deceive, things aren't what they seem,
and Hank was the rebel with a cause for destiny.
He got the nickname "Spike" as a goof from Grace,
when he took on the "Gypsy Jokers"
and put them in their place.
At eighteen, he'd seen it all, was well on his way.
His one wish, to be riding with the big boys at the bay.

Must have been in sixty five when I first met Spike,
sitting in his small garage, working on his bike.
He would snatch up and eat a moth as it hovered in the air, saying,
"A Biker's gotta be ready anytime, anywhere."
He'd eat that bug, a gaze in his eyes unknown,
like a badger to a bear saying, "Best leave me alone."
Jumping on his Harley, with a kick, he was gone.
I wondered what kind of trip this guy was on.

Stories have a way of changing in passing time,

fact and fiction seem to get mixed up as time goes by.
But I heard tell later on, while heading for some surf,
Spike was cruising slowly through Angel's turf.
If confrontation was his plan, well then he got his dare.
They stopped him asking why he was there.
As push comes to shove, as you know it always will,
Hank took up the challenge to race over the hill.
Hank didn't say nothing, but followed on their tail,
as the leader named Romeo started up the trail.
They stopped up by a cliff that had a wicked span,
Romeo said, "Here's where you show you're a man."
Spike, went down a ways and lurched on his ride,
hit the cliff at sixty-five and flew to the other side.
Circle-skidded to a stop, to view Their leader's sort,
but Romeo overconfident, fell off a might short.
It wasn't very long before Spike had got his way.
Riding with the Angels down by the Frisco bay.

Life on the biker's road is hard for someone new,
but nobody was telling Skelly how or what to do.
He had some biker Chick, holding on from behind,
she was a head taller, but He didn't pay it any mind.
Although he was smaller than the boys in the pack,
Hank held his own, nobody gave him any crap.
The wild, fast life moves, a biker's road is never done,
like wind in his hair, he loved being on the run.
The motorcycle maniac made the gray asphalt scream,
he never did look back when he made the scene.

Watch out for what you wish for, it might come true,
dreams can turn to nightmares before they're through.
Spike fell into hard times his Harley was old.
He knew he needed a new ride to keep up with the goals.
Then one day while cruising West Covina Hank spied

a loaded, 66, police Electro-Glide.
His eyes scanned the alley, seeing he was alone,
he was hot-wiring the ignition to take that baby home.
Meanwhile from the back of a bar stepping outside,
was officer Beagle seeing Hank stealing his ride.
Without a warning shot, without a warning said,
he shot down Hank Skelly in the back of the head.

Word got round quick, lines were drawn from hearsay,
but there wasn't much anyone could do anyway.
The inquest was a sham, Beagle pleaded self-defense
And even though he'd been drinking and didn't make much sense,
Hank Skelly was a rebel, a trouble maker on the street,
and in those days that was just as bad as being a minority.
Beagle, with no just cause, was let off with a smile,
though kicked off the force, he never did stand trial.

Hank's funeral, spoke of the young and brave,
two hundred bikers escorted the remains to the grave.
At the West Covina station they rode up in force,
"We'll trade you $7000 for Beagle and his horse."
Their answer came with riot guns, the Angels rode away,
with no pursuit by boys in blue, there was nothing left to say.
Days later, friends and family came from all around,
they buried Hank's Duo-Glide beside him in the ground.

You come and go, live and die shifting through life's gears
hoping to find purpose in you're time allotted here.
Hank had his problems, traveling highways that were curved,
some even say he got what he deserved.
But I think in biker's heaven, he just waits his turn,
for the second coming, and the time he will return.
I can see a Duo-Glide, stripped clean and made to go,
just Hank and his Harley, burning up the road.

99

Cruising While I'm Losing

I thought it didn't matter, when she left that night.
I just knew I was wrong but I had to be right.
I thought it didn't matter as I was so full of pride,
that I just gave up and took the long hard ride,
and I'm cruising, while I'm losing.
They'd say, ?Be a good sport?, well that's easy to say,
while they're sitting up there, looking down my way.
They'd say, ?Be a good sport, don't let it get you down?.
But I'm hitting the skids and it's all over town.
Still, I'm cruising, while I'm losing.
It must have been my fault, I acted kind of bad,
I did some foolish things and she left here mad.
It must have been my fault, still I didn't care,
till it was all too late and she left me there.
But I'm cruising, while I'm losing.
I'd like to turn things around, not just let it be,
but I don't think she wants to have anything to do with me.
I'd like to turn thing around, and be happy again
and I'm hoping to change, but until then
I'll be cruising, while I'm losing, I'm cruising, while I'm losing.

100

Shoes Are For The
Domesticated Feet

People sit at home conformed even though they have been warned.
They lie around from dusk till dawn, they sit until their life is gone.
And so I say these words so sweet, shoes are for domesticated feet.

T.V. dinners, machinery, swimming pools, false scenery.
People can't see through the walls, soon there won't be life at all.
They'll all be alive and still be dead,
Like America's sweetheart, they won't leave their bed.
There will be no people on the street,
and shoes are for domesticated feet.

No labor true, but what price to pay less work to do day by day
People can't read between the lines.
What ever happened to the brilliant minds?
Arms of muscle soon turn to fat.
Deep impressions are where they sat.
Life is a contest in which all compete
and shoes are for domesticated feet.

101

Running Away

A sandy beach, a trip upstate, a little peace, some time away.
Some other place, I just can't face things right now.
Jump in the car, reward myself,
head fast and far to someplace else.
Doesn't matter which way, I just can't stay around.
Running away from my problems,
need to lose this weight off my mind.
Trying to hide the reality by leaving it all behind.
What can I say, I just cant stay, so I'm running away.
Friends say I'm wrong to turn tail south.
The pressure is gone if I'd confront things now.
I just need time to get things right for me.
A small resort, a chance to change,
a leave of sort from feeling so strange.
Get away and about, to work things out at my own speed.
Running away from my problems,
need to lose this weight off my mind.
Trying to hide the reality by leaving it all behind.
What can I say? After feeling this way,
I just cant stay,... I'm running away.

102

The Mud Puddle

When it rains and the sun won't shine,
I go to a place that is mine, all mine.
A place where I can get away from the race,
I kneel down and look at my face
in the mud puddle, in the mud puddle.
Raindrops falling in the muddy water deep.
White worms crawling, in the puddle they'll creep.
So clean and white, they'll soon turn brown.
It's so strange, I think I'll go down
to the mud puddle, to the mud puddle.
I take off my shoes and step inside,
it covers them over like they're trying to hide.
So clean and white, they'll soon turn brown,
it's so strange, I think I'll go down
to the mud puddle, to the mud puddle.
In the mud puddle.

103

One Day At A Time

They say in time, things will get easier
but they haven't yet
I'm still waiting for the change.
Though years have passed,
I still fight an empty. Lonely. way things get
with your love out of range.
Not much has changed,
I still cherish all the things we both held dear
before you had to go.
I know that you must have a good reason for leaving here
but what it is I still don't know.

Still, I live my life one day at a time.
I draw lines setting goals I know, I'll never reach or find.
I live my life one day at a time,
and I do fine, until your memory crosses my mind.

Our little Anne turned five the other day, She asked me why
her mother never calls.
I still get urged to go out and have some fun before I die

behind these same four walls.
I guess my wish is you'll be coming home to us any day,
but that's like wishing on a star.
The sad truth is, I've no place to send this letter anyway,
because I don't know where you are.

Still, I live my life one day at a time.
I draw lines making goals I know, I'll never reach or find.
I live my life one day at a time,
and I'll do fine, until your memory crosses my mind.

104

Just Another Bimmy - No. 1

Well it's time to go and you might think so,
when I tell you about the way that I spend my day.
Because I'm washing plates and it's what I hate.
I'm just another Bimmy, from another city.
A day late and dollar short, half sick from too much port.
A tapped city jerk and looking for work.
Well I drink my beer just to keep in gear,
but a little Jack Daniels and I fly off the handle.
Well I'm just another Bimmy, from another city.
Trying to find a better way but all I get is another bus tray.
Sorting through knishes just to find my dishes.
I ain't worried about what is fair, because I just don't care.
as long as sometime today I'll go pick up my pay.
I'm just another Bimmy, from another city.
So it's time to go and now you know why
I sort through the trash for some extra cash.
Every man must uncover everything he can discover.
And you know it's a pity when you're getting all gritty,
but I'm just another Bimmy, from another city.

105

Don't Make Me Beg For Your Love

What is it that you seem to try to hide?
I feel something deep inside.
I'm tired of being on the schnide.
Baby, don't make me beg for your love.
Please, don't make me beg for your love.
Are you just tightening up your grip,
or do you like to see me squirm just to be whipped?
Go ahead and play out your trip,
Baby, but don't make me beg for your love.
Please, don't make me beg for your love.
Baby, don't make me beg for your love.
I know that things have been real tough,
and I'm the one that made things seem so rough.
Maybe it seems like I never get enough,
but Baby, don't make me beg for your love.
Please! Don't make me beg for your love —not Tonight!!
Don't make me beg for your love.

106

‾‾‾‾‾‾‾‾‾

MEMOIRS & NOTES - 07 - 'TAKING ME FOR A RIDE

Taking Me For A Ride

(Written 1984) – At this point, for more clarification of some of my material written between 1984 & 1985, I have to mention in some detail, my friend, Darryl Wade, who worked as the *other* gravedigger at the Forest Memorial Gardens' Cemetery. Darryl was the son of Jerry Wade who was one of the two owners of the funeral home, and because of such, Darryl was always under the scrutinizing eyes of Gary Rook, the Managing Funeral Director who was eternally paranoid that Darryl was spying on him and the general operations for his father. Darryl came in on a recommendation from his father, who wanted his son to be working and to temporarily replace the last gravedigger, Rick, who had left.

Rick was slow, thick, and gullible, and in the end, except for Gary, hard to get along with; there was a 50/50 chance that anybody replacing him was going to be better.

Darryl was a "lost soul" kind of guy; in between odd jobs and pushed by his father into this provisional arrangement. The reason I mention Darryl is that his enthusiasm and compelling encouragement did more to promote and accelerate my songwriting than anybody else, before or since. He would come into the office to take a break after digging a grave, covered with cemetery dirt, and he would sit down on one of the lounge chairs in the outer office where I seconded as the receptionist/ typist, and he would light up a smoke and talk.

One day he came in while I was plunking away on a beat-up guitar and was decidedly impressed. I told him that I had just written that tune and he asked if I had anything else. When he found out that I had this folder with over 100 poems in it, he insisted on listening to every song. Afterwards he formed his own opinions of his own favorite selections, which I ended up playing over and over again. After that encounter, he would come in often for his breaks, every time expecting me to entertain him with something new, and I usually did.

What made this arrangement so pleasant was his apparent love for my raw but potential talent and exceptional material. It was like everything I did had a promise of excellence if I would just reach a bit further, so I rose to the occasion and raised my bar of ability to accommodate his expectations. But it was his encouragement, his excitement over my work, and his unmitigated believe that I could do something with my songs that drove me forward; made me rise to the occasion and be as good, and better, as Darryl's expectations were.

Although to me this song had a catchy tune and snappy lyrics, to me, it was really nothing special; but Darryl thought this song had good potential for commercial exploitation. So, I worked hard to pull the strings in and tighten the song up. The effect at the time was great, and back in 1985 I could also belt this out a lot better than I can now— it had this tempo that kind of made you want to sing-along. Not necessarily being gullible and being drawn around by the nose, this song is perhaps more about thinking twice before jumping into something that has possible damaging, long-range or lasting negative ramifications.

The Ballad of Hank Skelly

(Written 1968) - The words to this poem come from a real-life character that I knew from my 60s Los Angeles days. The essence of this character is tightly based on reality with some liberties taken from the urban-legend folklore tales I pieced together after my release from the Los Angeles J.D.H. in the fall of 1967. The words tell the story of a small in stature, perhaps rather thick-skinned but warmhearted young man who's concentrated and most sought-after ambition in life was to become one of the Hell's Angels. It is my hope after I finish these "Words For Songs" documents to edit and publish his personification in my book, **"Heads, or Tales From the Summer of Love."** The essence of this song was created on a Friday night in February of 1968 in a 56 Buick, full of stoned-out high school hippies traveling from Brown's Mills, New Jersey to New York City to see the best acid trip movie of all times, "2001, A Space Odyssey." The radio didn't work in the car and it was an hour's drive from Fort Dix to the City. We were talking about some of our war and peace stories from the past summer and I started telling the story about a Californian I knew named Hank Skelly. It wasn't all at once or suddenly, but somewhere past Morristown I realized the whole vehicle was completely silent as everyone hung on to my every word. It was a power that intoxicated me like no drug could ever do. Seeing I had this captive audience and this big time-frame to work with, I did a "Purple Grotto" rendition, embellishing the story with some of the quirky characteristics of Hank, some of my best friends Tim and Randy, as well as the two motorcycle gangs Hank was involved with, as well as some other friends and other characters from those Glendora California times. As I approached the end of the story, I said; Hank wasn't the kind of guy anyone would like, but he lived and died a biker with his 54 duo-glide. I then pulled out my harmonica and did a small blues refrain. With a kind of folklore or urban legend feel to it, I concluded the story and then did a repeat, but longer rendition of that blues refrain on my harmonica. When I finally finished playing and put my harmonica away, we were somewhere between Jersey City and Hoboken, looking for the Holland Tunnel. On the way back home that night I was asked to do a repeat of the "Ballad of Hank Skelly," which I did, and probably did a better job the second time around, but except for 'Moby' the driver, everyone else had long since crashed. When I went back to school the following Monday, my reputation preceded me and I was not only asked to repeat the ballad, but I was inducted into a local group without them even hearing me tell the story or play my harmonica. It didn't last though, as school and my independence ended with a summer job up in the Catskills. This poetic but up-tempo rendition of the piece lacks the melodramatic feel I had when I recited the story in 1968, and the harmonica on this piece is too upbeat to carry the feel of the impending disaster that was about to befall Hank. Still, I rather liked this first recorded rendition of" The *Ballad of Hank Skelly*" because of the driving sounds of the funky 80s Casio keyboard and its percussion accompaniment as well as the rhyming lyrics and harmonica interludes, which at the time seemed to have a kind of we're-out-on-the-open-road feel.

Cruising, While I'm Losing

(Written 1991) – This is another of the many poems written during my lunch hour at the Parks Department. Many of the poems like this one were written in a 30 to 45-minute span of time. My thought when writing this poem was that we can believe or convince ourselves just about anything after a relationship has been terminated, but we have to know that the truth is, sometimes we are the cause for the resulting hurt, and although we've come to understand it was the wrong thing to do, in hindsight, we end up having to live with the results of our actions. Many of the words to the poems were rushed and, of course, would sometimes compromise the initial products, but not this one. From the beginning, the words flowed easily and when the marriage to the music took place, I knew it was something special. My next indication was running it by my teenagers who mildly but collectively endorsed the song. My final acid test was to leave it alone and come back to it a while later. Over time I have found that sometimes, what turned me on at first, turned out to be less than later or even nominal, and then ended up in the "C" basket, (categorizing the songs by what I felt was an "A" "B" or "C" song, depending on its appeal, its lyrics and music exceptionalism), but this one stayed true from it's inception and has remained so since, maintaining its special magic.

Shoes Are For The Domesticated Feet

(Written 1968) – This is one of my oldest surviving poems in my collection. I wrote this at Pemberton-Township High School in Pemberton, New Jersey. After being stricken helpless, overwhelmed by Bob Dylan's work, I spent many of my mandatory study periods writing poems and lyrics for songs that, after spacing a bit of time between readings, were far to plagiaristic and similar to his work to do anything with. But they were all good practice vehicles to the progression of my writings. Most of these "exercises" or "practices" have disappeared through the years, but some of my free-write works that were original *and*, not crap managed to survive. This poem is a call to nonconformity and a realization that there is a price we all pay for everything in our lives; even technology and industrialization hold strong pressures for more changes that sometimes works against us as a whole as well as individually. In my high-school days of the late 60s there was a movement to be conscientious of the political world around us as well as being a critical thinker, (yes, sounds kind of like the **Hippy** movement, but in fact, the **Beat** movement preceded the **Hippy** movement and let's not forget Socrates). And sometimes, perhaps like Huckleberry Finn, to be a non-conformist. The lyrics to this poem denote awareness to a changing social norm and thus, is a stand of awareness and a possible move against that whirlpool of placid acceptance to the powers that were or perhaps maybe still are that would subjugate our existence for the gain, money, power, influence of, to or against others.

Running Away

(Written 1986) – The Buddha (also known as Siddhartha Gautama), arguably the founder of Buddhism, in his struggle for the meaning of life, become an ascetic, or wandering holy man, and he spent his life teaching "*The Four Noble Truths*." The *first truth* is that all existence is full of suffering. The *second truth* is that suffering arises from the constant effort to find comfort and stability in an uncertain world. Who wants to suffer or confront adversity in an unstable and uncertain world?

After the funeral home was sold in the fall of 1985, I wandered aimlessly for a short time looking for work before getting an offer and going back to work at J W Electronics. Going back to a place I'd left because I was fired, was not easy for me. There were many individuals that were elated when I left and I was sure they would be rolling their eyes when I returned. Moreover, there were some individuals that I felt the need to "mend fences" with before I started working there. I don't think I ever experienced a greater, more stressful anxiety than the Friday evening that I spent calling up all these people that had been mean to me, and there were some that just didn't like me. And so I called each one of these individuals, asking for some type of viable or at least temporary truce at work. In some cases, I knew I needed to ask for forgiveness for my past transgressions, knowing, that regardless of what their reactions were, I would nonetheless, be facing them the following Monday.

There was this person named Donny, that, on hearing me announce who I was, immediately hung up on me. I called him back, thinking it was a fluke or something, and then, as he reluctantly allowed me to speak, I asked Donny for forgiveness for whatever it was than had caused a rift in out relationship. But, perhaps because he had been prejudiced by my being the incompetent son-in-law of the owner, or perhaps because, from the time I started working there, I had shied away from or never joined the beer-drinking comradery of workers there, or perhaps from his loyalty to others there that didn't take a shine to me either, whatever the reason, he quickly and flatly said "No."

In hopes of clarifying what I thought was a mistake, I said, "What?"

He strongly returned with another, "No." and then he said strongly, but with a voice void of emotion, "I don't like you and I will do what

I can to get you fired again" and then he hung up. It was during that weekend, in between the times the calls were made, that I began writing the words to this poem which would get buried away and reexamined and then rewritten about two or three months later, after I got acclimated and somewhat comfortable again at my job there. Although I made the calls and weathered all the differing results, I was the one that wanted to do something else—anything else but confront those people and my problems—I was the one that wanted to be Running Away.

The Mud Puddle

(Written 1973) – In 1973 there was still a large intolerance for interracial marriages, even in the Pacific Northwest where I considered the problems to be minimal. I decided to do a "what if" and take a walk on the wild side. Still, can racial and ethnic incorporation or integration save America from its cultural problems? These were thoughts that I had at the time that I wrote this piece, masked by allegoric rhetoric and a cool harmonica riff. This is one of those poems I composed loosely one evening while jamming over at Louie's apartment and then later that evening or to be precise, on into the morning, I put together this song. The chords were designed to invoke a harmonica to be played in small parts during the hesitating interims of the stanzas and then in detail, in between the verses. I had given Louie a harmonica months earlier for him to learn, and he was still in the beginning stages, but this song, (done in "E" major, using an "A" harmonica) called out to the blues in one's soul and Louie wasn't quite ready to hear from his musical psyche and it would be many years later before I recorded this song and unfortunately, what I wanted and what I captured were still two different musical and philosophical things.

One Day At A Time

(Written 1986) – My database indicates that this was composed in 1986, but for some reason I'm remembering this in the Summer of 1985.

Neither here nor there, I put together the words to this poem one evening after Diane and I had one of her single adult friends over for dinner. I empathized with our guest and the trials that she was going through at that time. Later I put together the words in the tune, and I wasn't really happy with the way things turned out. One weekend our family went camping at the Margaret McKenney campground with our kids, and after everyone had gone to sleep, I grabbed my guitar went out in the open field and worked on the song. At the time I also had another tune, an instrumental that I was playing with that was in its early stages of creation. That evening, I transposed the song from the key of C to D and inadvertently put the instrumental and the song together. I kind of liked the results and that's how it stayed.

Side Note:

A while later, the Olympia/Lacey area was visited by Marie Osmond who was doing a kind of Country and Western concert at the St. Martin's Pavilion in Lacey. Of all the people that I had profiled to do this song; she was at the top of the list. I envisioned her singing this with a sad, melancholy voice that would bring tears to everyone's eyes. I prepared for a week, getting up my nerve and material together, writing down the lyrics, recording the music, and putting it altogether in a nice package, to present to her. That night, after the concert was over, along with hundreds of other LDS kids, I went backstage and got a chance to hand this package to her. Her bodyguard stood between me and her as she smiled; *oh, and it was a very hopeful smile*, before she said, "I'll listen to this and I'll get back to you." I know, I know... right? I should not have expected that my material was so good that Marie Osmond would immediately pop the tape into her boombox and play it, and then rush out after me to make arrangements to have the song recorded, right? Well, I did stay outside her door for at least another 20 minutes before I noticed all the band equipment was leaving as well as most of the cars and trucks in the parking lot and realized that everyone inside that other door had left from other interior doors. Still, I held onto that dream of her or one of her people calling me the next day; the next week; the next month; I never heard from her again, and I imagined (or realized) that the clunking sound I had heard that night as the door shut behind her was the package (and my dream) going directly into the garbage can without ever been examined or even opened. And like I said, I went through a period of hopefulness, thinking that maybe she would find some time and listen to it and realize it was the chance of a lifetime, song, but as time went on, my cynicism crept in, along with doubt and eventually annoyance. "How could she just not even listen to it?" I thought, judging her and her squeaky white character. Then my ego reported, "this song could have put her right on top." From there I went to a dark place with thoughts of extracting revenge in the near future when I became rich and famous, but, I eventually I got over it. I Still perform this song a lot and if nothing else, it makes me happy to know that over the years since that happening, the responsive sound and the sensitivity of the poignant, emotional feel of the song has never diminished. That alone brings me a sense of peace and closure to the whole event.

Just Another Bimmy - No. 1

(Written 1977) – From the database perspective this poem was written 1977, but in fact most of the words to this poem were actually written in 1971 by my brother Richard. He was working at Charlou's, a small restaurant in Monticello New York, washing dishes, bussing and cleaning tables and counters and other menial tasks. It was at that time and from his experiences that this song or to be precise the words to this poem were created. Years later during one of our jam sessions, Richie brought this song out. I was thoroughly intrigued by the whole thing, the meter, the colorful words, and most especially, the concept of the song itself. I put music to it and we all had a good laugh doing it.

Side Note:

As a little brief history; the word "Bimmy" in the late '50s and early '60s denoted east-coast immigrant, Puerto Ricans, Cubans, and people of color that worked in the kitchens as cooks, aids, dishwashers and groundskeepers for the hotels in the Catskills. Somewhere in the middle of the '60s the term, "Bimmy" loosely took on an inclusive meaning to denote any person that was doing the unskilled, lowly, monotonous and mind-numbing jobs or those particular types of work. Richie, who one summer had taken this lowlife job himself as a dishwasher, was now working with other lowlifes, and for all given purposes, had become a Bimmy himself. Being considered or considering yourself to be a lowlife in the land of the brave and the home of the free was an interesting concept to me and I took the words from his lyrics, and embellished his words and included some of my own, especially to make the rhyming work better. After Richie heard my version and compared it with the original words of his poem, he decided to take a few of the ideas that I had and incorporate them into his own work.

Still, there was something, a mood, a feel, I don't know, I couldn't capture the essence without returning to the originality of the whole thing.

Second Side Note:

This cool song was recorded as version 1, which is the purest interpretation of the original poem that Richie wrote back in 1971.

Don't Make Me Beg For Your Love

(Written 1992) – Love is good and can be a motivating factor to get things done, but no one wants or should be held hostage in a relationship, especially to someone on the schnide like the protagonist in this poem. This was another one of those poems that I wrote during my unemployment times, in between jobs. The chords to the song were in a simple progression and I took the rhythm in an easy flowing meter. The voice was to be from someone feeling the need to get love while the other, is holding out. As the song progresses, there is s growing anxiety to the protagonist till it all but explodes with the final and desperate scream, "*Please.*"

Side Note A:

I had a bad cold when I originally recorded the vocals to this song, (as well as the song, **"One Day At A Time"**), and the effect from my voice for both songs was kind of cool.

Side Note B:

After the song was finished, I envisioned Eric Clapton doing this song, embellishing the areas, just past the choruses as well as at the end of the song, by him adding the crusty guitar riffs that I was incapable of playing at the time. To me, this song seems to rise **above** most of the other songs on the album, almost to the point that it doesn't fit—but then, as the last song, it's almost perfect in an album called, *"Taking Me For A Ride."*

107

08 - EVER ON - 1992

108

⚜

NOTES ABOUT THE
COVERS

I knew that I needed original art for my albums, but the original cover for this album, Ever On, (Seen below) had, "The Creation of Adam" on the cover. Being a true believer, I felt that this cover could be a light, (however bright), to others out there and maybe draw good people to listen to the album. It was one of the covers that did not pass the inspectors, who notified me that the cover had been rejected.

I would have thought that with so much time gone by since Michelangelo painted the Sistine Chapel, (1508) that intellectual property would be long past. I found out that A Japanese TV network (NHK) stepped forward and paid between $3 and $4 Million for the "Inglorious Restorations". The Vatican could only license the copyrights of a public domain work due to an old quirk of copyright law. The original artwork may be in the public domain, but a photograph of that artwork, any exclusive film and publication rights may be copyrighted as a new unique work.

So instead, I took a still of a trip to the Westport State Park Beach, which was part of one of our family campouts. It pictures much of my family walking to the ocean with shadows in the sand and the differences between the ocean and the sky seems to fade into itself. This new cover was a good substitute for Michelangelo's interpretation of, "The Creation of Adam" with families can be forever,... **Ever On**

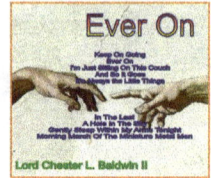

109

EVER ON

Keep On Going
Ever On
Sitting Here On This Couch
And So It Goes
It's Always the Little Things
In The Last
A Hole In The Sky
Gently Sleep-
Within My Arms Tonight

110

Keep On Going

Seems I'm fighting just to wrestle my way out of a sack.
I take one step forward and three steps back.
But I know how it goes I won't admit defeat.
Everyone knows they can depend on me.
To keep on going, to keep on going.
You might slow me down enough to pause,
but you can't stop a man with a cause, to keep on going.
Seems I got the whole world pushing me back.
I got all these distractions to make me jump track.
I have to struggle to get through and I'm under the gun,
but I got a job to do and I get the job done.
To keep on going, to keep on going.
I've got an open mind and a clear head,
with my sights aimed straight ahead to keep on going.
I might not always seem to have enough,
but the tough get going when the going gets tough,
to keep on going.

Ever On

Although it flickers and wanes
the light of my love remains
burning ere,
forever on.
Although the times lay heavy on us now,
with the love that we've made
we can make it somehow.
We're turning ere,
forever on.
Although mistakes come and go we have our share,
we live and we learn
and go on from there.
We're learning ere,
but it's forever on.
Although the roads leave mountains to climb,
my love knows no distance
and no concepts of time.
We're journeying ere,
and it's forever on.

112

Sitting Here On This Couch

I have tried so hard to become what I should be,
I've forgotten who I was, or what I believe.
I walk the streets of uselessness searching for work and pay.
Talking to personnel robots saying they got nothing today.
But I'm just sitting on this couch, doing with little or without.
Eating dinner, watching TV, trying to shake all these doubts.
Hey, hey, I'm just sitting on this couch,
it's a much easier way out.
Doing nothing at all, but sitting here on this couch.
My light burns twice as bright, but half as long.
So I stayed up at night to devote to some new song.
I go through the motions that I do each day so well.
Nobody seems to needs me now
but next week who can tell?
I'm just sitting on this couch, doing with little or without.
Eating dinner, watching the reruns,
and the kids all running about.
I'm just sitting on this couch, it's a much easier way out.
And I'm a, doing nothing at all, but sitting here on this couch.
Yeah, I got a pillow under my head; I'm pretty comfortable.

I's a trying to find where I fit, to carry my life through.
There's no illusions or lies, I know what I can do.
I got my dreams of how these things might go some day;
I just haven't figured out how to make it work that way.
So, I'm just sitting on this couch, doing with little or without.
Eating dinner, watching TV, I don't care what it's all about. Hey,
you know I'm just sitting on this couch,
it's a much easier way out.
And I'm a, a doing nothing at all, but sitting here on this couch.

113

And So It Goes

And so it goes,
the spirit has left the knowing eyes.
Though it doesn't show,
this passing begins a new life.
And on and on and on and on it goes.
The still, lifeless hand
is hard to give into the night.
Yet, to understand
that darkness gives way to new light.
And on and on and on and on it goes.
Time touches the friend with a passing of kin,
but though one path ends, another begins,
and on and on and on and on it goes.
And so it goes,
this cycle as sunset meets dawn.
Eternally flows
to progress through unknown and beyond.
And on and on and on and on it goes.
On and on and on and on it goes.

114

Always The Little Things

We've gotten separated, now we just don't talk.
Something's missing from those eyes, that seem so sad and lost.
You've got your reasons why, Honey, I've got mine,
but we'll go down the drain if we never cross the line.
It's always the little things that tear us apart.
Little words that hurt you more and always breaks your heart.
It's always the little things that bring us out of touch.
Not much alone, but added up little things become too much.
Am I the one, or is it you, or a little bit of both,
that carries on this stupid game no one will win at all.
If it was something I felt guilty for, I'd gladly take the fall,
but I just feel so out of place and confused by it all.
It's always the little things that tear us apart.
Little words that hurt you more and always breaks your heart.
It's always the little things that bring us out of touch.
Not much alone, but added up little things become too much.
Things said, or things not said, the actions good or bad,
and all the little attitudes just break down what we have.
We've always worked things out before
and did the best we could,

I'd like to think that we might still have something good.
It's always the little things that tear us apart.
Little words that hurt you more and always breaks your heart.
It's always the little things that bring us out of touch.
Not much alone, but added up little things become too much.

115

In The Last

In the last, looking at my life,
woven within the lines, the colors and designs
have all remained.
In the last, I see the real disease,
a prideful part of me and yet I had to be
self contained.
In the last, for now, I still recall
the passion of it all, to climb the hill and wall
to meet my test.
In the last, through failures I once grieved,
the goals never achieved, but ones who still believed
in my quest.
And though it never finally happened,
it's too late to deny or defend.
It never really mattered, just a means to an end.
In the last, I followed all the trails,
watched their dreams set sails, while a carpenter with nails
must work the day.
In the last, remembering back when,
ambitions I had then, what might or should have been

all slip away.
And though it never really happened,
it's too late to deny or defend.
In the end, it never mattered, just a means to an end.

116

❦

A Hole In The Sky

The city fathers thought to accommodate more cars,
they'd turn the freeway route
through my Grandmother's backyard.
They forced the sale of the homes with no choice but must,
the place under construction looked like a bomb dropped on us.
Now there's a hole in the sky,
that will always look different from my eyes.
when I think of those good times gone by, there's a hole in the sky.
Cats leveled down the house to a pile of rocks,
and the basement was filled with chunks of the old sidewalk.
Yet the worst thing was my two-hundred-year-old friend,
the giant Black Cherry Tree that they sawed up in the end.
Now, there's a hole in the sky,
that will always look different from my eyes.
when I think of those good times gone by, there's a hole in the sky.
With my brothers, we'd climb the limbs to eat our fill,
or lay down on the garage roof and just eat till we got ill.
An old lawn swing was sheltered by it's shade,
as we were off on safari, or in the Sherwood forest glade.
Now, there's a hole in the sky

that will always look different from my eyes.
when I think of those good times gone by, there's a hole in the sky.
Old ninety sixth street will never be the same.
Too many years passed before they finished their monopoly game.
Don't know what happened to all my friends down the street,
but the block didn't make the freeway,
just an off-ramp short and sweet.
Now, there's a hole in the sky
that will always look different from my eyes.
when I think of those good times gone by, there's a hole in the sky.

117

Gently Sleep Within My
Arms Tonight

The castle safe in setting sun, a noble peace indeed.
With sword now sheathed and kingdom won,
a good rest is in need.
Dragons and children have all gone to sleep.
Finally, we're all alone, one promise left to keep.
A twilight kiss under the stars to spark this love alight,
and gently sleep within my arms tonight.

With vanquished foes, your prince in debt
for damsel in distress.
Together walk the blue sunset, forever happiness.
Happy ever-after, in love we'll always stay.
A knowing glance, a warm embrace as all else slips away.
A twilight kiss under the stars to spark this love so right,
and gently sleep within my arms tonight.

No questions asked, all is right, know what I'm thinking of.
In peace and quiet of the night, you radiate in love.

Dragons and children have all gone to sleep.
Finally, we're all alone, one promise left to keep.
A twilight kiss under the stars to spark this love alight,
and gently sleep within my arms tonight.

118

◦⨓◦

MEMOIRS & NOTES - 08 - 'EVER ON'

Keep On Going

(1991) – This was another one of my songs written for Johnny Cash, or at least with him in mind. At the time that this poem was written, Johnny Cash was involved with a partnership with Willie Nelson, Kris Kristofferson and Waylon Jennings forming a group called, "The Highwaymen." Of course, by this time Johnny was close to 60 years old, but I thought to myself, that I might be able to write him a big hit, where tenacity, determination and persistence in pursuing his dreams and goals, (which is, of course, what the poem is all about), and he could climb right back on top again, and I could be discovered. Well as I stated before, this song, as well as other songs, never got to him or anyone else for that matter. But nonetheless, at the time prospects and the dream excited me. And after all, the song was good enough for me and sustained my hope. Although that hope of a possible future in the music business never materialized, it kept me going.

Side Note:

I should begin by apologizing to Lori for how hard it must have been for her with me as copilot, and her being the first in line of so many wanting to get their drivers licenses, and me not knowing how or what I was doing to do as a driving instructor, but coming from the other direction, I would be the one that would have to face certain death teaching her how to drive.

Lori was not happy to have to learn how to drive in the extended Plymouth Voyager van, (albeit she was driving down the road in a beast of a vehicle that was nearly seven feet high, six and a half feet wide and over 16 feet long) we lovingly called, "the Green Pickle" but it was all we had that had an automatic gearbox so she didn't need to know how to use a clutch. And yes, she was taking driver's training at the high school, but to her, this driver's training class was yet another opportunity to socialize with her friends, and I'm sure that they weren't paying any attention to what the other student drivers were doing right or wrong; this was a like a glorified hayride to them as each student or friend took their turn at frightening the school instructor to death as they sallied on down the road. But think about me, having my life continually being put in jeopardy as she casually say's "whoops," as she slams on the breaks nearly sending me through the windshield, or when she laughs nervously as she climbs up over some curb with the back tire after negotiating her turn too sharply, or her disregard for any instruc-tions like, "Slow down or you'll hit that car in front of you!" where she would brake but pretend she was already on it. At times, if she felt I was mistaken or like assuming to herself that I'm being over cautious, she would politely ignore me. And Lori has a lead foot, which arguably is needed with the van on the freeway, but she drove way too fast in the wrong places, causing me to constantly ask, "didn't they teach you that at school?" with an ambiguous or flippant answer, "Yeah, so?" The thing I hated the most was Lori's ability to choose from all the things I would tell her and accept only what she felt was in her belief system.

Second Side Note:

This was an agonizing experience that I shared with Diane as we alternated co-piloting, and to be fair, it could not have been easy on Lori to go through this rite of passage, to have pioneer the way for her oncoming brothers and sisters, but think about her humble parents that offered up their lives for the sake of their children's need to be socially acceptable and be able to pull out and flash that driver's license around as they would walk down the school hallways. In the end, she got her license and would take the van on many journeys that, for reasons of confidentiality, we still have not heard of yet.

Ever On

(1972) – One day in 1985, while working on an obituary and a death certificate at the funeral home, my friend Darryl, the makeshift gravedigger, came into the receiving area of the funeral home, sat down in a chair next to me, and told me that I was going to be recording some of my material in a recording studio.

The story as I remember it happening went like this; Darryl was in a bar drinking with friends and the subject came up about one of his friends that was a songwriter. Over a gamble, (from the winner of a pool game), bets were made and things were wagered, and somehow, Darryl walked out of that bar with two free sessions at this guy's recording studio, which was located not too far out, off of Cooper-Point Road.

I was, to say the least, blown over. No one had ever done anything like that for me before. I scrambled, looking over all my material, trying to figure out just what my best songs might be. I came up with a couple different ideas, tested some select pieces of my material, and after I kicked a few things around the block, I ended up doing this song here.

Down a dirt road, off the main highway, buried in the trees, the recording studio was in a large barn-like garage. It had an 8-track console recording device with a lot of whistles and bells as well as other cool equipment and stuff everywhere.

I brought my 1963-64 Fender King acoustic guitar to a shop and paid $40 to have the bridge fixed, to take out the buzz. When I arrived, I still hadn't decided which song to do, and played about an hour for a young guy named, "Stony," who was the producer, director, engineer and owner of the recording studio. It was decided that we would record three songs and this song, Ever On, would be the first. This song had me singing a two-part harmony, with a voice over on the main lead. I also added some keyboard work that gave a flute-like tone to the music and at the end, I had the music march back in, reiterating the little tune, accompanied with a background of a distant harmonica.

Side Note:

The recording turned out great and everyone I played the tape for afterwards could not believe that it was me and my song they were listening to. I was in heave and working on what song would be next. Unfortunately, less than a month after I recorded this song, someone backed up a truck to the doors of the bard studio and took everything inside, including my master tape, one of my microphones, and all my hopes and dreams of recording the two other songs.

Second Side Note:

Curiously, although this song was recorded in the studio and all the other songs on the album were not, it strangely fits in with everything else. This love poem that I wrote for Diane back in 1972 still holds some of the magic and the wonder of what I was trying to say about our relationship in our love and my devotion to her.

Sitting Here On This Couch

(1974) – One evening, probably in the late 70s sometime, I was over at Ray's house, doing a few of my regular old standby tunes and Ray said, "Let's do that song you played last time you were down here. Let's play, Sitting On The Couch next." I searched my mental database, which at the time was all there in my mind, but I found that this song was not in my head.

When I got back up in Olympia, I searched through my music closet, then through all of my paperwork, and even through all of my notes that I had strewn throughout the music cabinets. I could not find the song, Sitting On The Couch. It was then that I realized that there was a problem with my filing system, and it was then that I realized that there was a possibility that not only this song, but who knows how may other songs have been lost or gone missing because of my failure to document or at least to remember. I thought, "If I'm only 20 something now, and I'm losing songs, I better do something to ensure the fact that this will never happen again."

From that moment, I scrutinized all of my work and everything I wrote down was put in special places so that I could come back to them and re-work them at a later time. I don't know why it is that when I look at these words for songs I can almost always recall how the tune goes to it, but I'm thankful for this gift and blessing to be able to have this sense of certain recall. luckily, over the years I have managed to pull out the lyrics to many of the obscure songs and re-familiarize myself with them. This also gives me an edge at keeping things organized in my own head.

Side Note:

At the time I rewrote the song, (renamed), Sitting Here On This Couch, in 1990 after I had just lost my job, when JW Electronics went out of business. I was in between jobs, dealing with the problems and mindset of living the life of the unemployed, living on unemployment insurance. It was probably a good time to rewrite the song because I was in that certain frame of mind that you only get when you're there, destitute, down and out and unemployed. An added benefit to the rewriting of this song was my inclusion of a family that surrounded and supported me in my time of instability and uncertainty. The original song, Sitting On The Couch, with its tales of bureaucratic, nightmarish interactions with the world of the unsympathetic employed, could not have been more accurate than this one. And I love the seemingly phenomenal harmonica that I included at the end of this song, show-casing, what I believe to be, a precarious hope-against-hope feeling.

Second Side Note:

It would seem, after my magnanimous and dauntless efforts to recreate this song, that Ray would have been impressed and happy to play this song again. As I remember though, as I reintroduced the song to him, (and Richie and Charlie), Ray was somewhat indifferent to the song, not being what he'd remembered from the past and with that lack of enthusiasm, we never pulled this song out again to jam on. On a different note, Richie seemed to like the song a lot.

And So It Goes

(1988) – When we first got on the farm, Richie and I were a bit much for what was already happening there. We found that my dad was now married to a woman named Inez, and, because we had had no communications with my dad for years, we had never been made aware that we had two sisters, Wendy, maybe 13 at the time and Kathy maybe seven or eight. Also, there was this little four-and-a-half-foot-tall woman living there too, Inez's mother, soon to be known lovingly as Grandma Wicks.

It was already a small farm house with only three bedrooms and I won't get into too much about the farm and farm life right now, but needless to say, the house was small and there was no bedroom to put Richie and I into, so my dad decided to put us in a small, five-foot wide by seven-foot-long linen closet with a slanting, six-foot ceiling. And after we put a 28-inch wide by 60-inch long by 58-inch-high army bunk bed in it, Richie and I had barely enough room to get in and out of the small space.

Even though Grandma Wicks was not really our grandmother, when we moved into and onto the farm, she not only came with that total farm package, but she nonetheless, treated Richie and I like we were her long-lost grandsons. It wasn't very long before I knew that she indeed did love me. This small, woman, opened up her heart to interact with and care for me in a way that puzzled me. Because of her sweet and kind disposition, she enhanced my perspective of the hereafter and life after death.

And so, with her passing a few years later, I was left with a hole in my heart. It was because of her that this song with all its marvel was written. Perhaps as mentioned before, in 1992, my son Christopher Michael passed away in an unfortunate accident in Black Lake, Olympia. One of the things that I felt I needed to do was to sing this song at Christopher's services. But going through the grieving process, I realized that there was no way that I would be able to sing at my son's funeral.

As that moment got closer, I went over to the house of one of my kid's teachers from Black Lake Elementary who had his own recording studio with keyboards and guitars in his house. And after many stabs at it, breaking down repeatedly, I managed to record this song. Afterwards, or at least for the first few days before the services, I changed my mind and decided to sing the song. I felt it was what I had to do, knowing that it would take on a far greater meaning to be able to be brave and sing this song.

I thought I was prepared, but then the thought of getting up there in front of everyone and the fear of emotionally breaking down was just too much for me, and in the end, I made arrangements to have this recording played through the PA system at the services.

Side Note:

One of the things that I did was to incorporate one of my instrumentals; '*Dorothy's Song*' (named after a good friend, Dorothy Bradford), into this song, And So It Goes. The result was, in my opinion, effective and moving.

Second Side Note:

Putting together this album at the time, after Chris's passing, was a difficult task. I hardly felt like eating, much less playing and recording music, but I found the strength in the weeks ahead to finish the album. Some of the songs on this album were recorded prior to, during, and right after the funeral. But I found that the music and the creation of songs had a strong healing factor to it, and to my then damaged psyche.

Moreover, I discovered that the music comforted my soul so much so that my recording and writing capabilities accelerated, opening up the possibilities and creation of seven new albums (and many, many new songs), before the end of 1992.

This excruciating experience of losing one of your dear children; I would never wish upon anyone. I have heard the adage, time heals all wounds, but it's been years and I can say, that's not totally true. I do thank my Heavenly Father for the wonderful way music was able to comfort me in my time of need and help bring me to a better place in my life.

It's Always The Little Things

(1992) – Money matters seem to have an ability of galvanizing a relationship, made only more acutely aware when considering a couple that is already having financial problems, or are in financially embarrassing circumstances. From all the disagreements I've ever had with Diane, I'm guessing 80 percent, no, probably 90 percent of the disputes had something to do with money or the lack thereof. Love can be motivated by positive acceptance and mutual teamwork in the relationship, but if there are problems in communication or trust, things fall apart fast, and most of the time, it's usually something trivial or small.

If you think about it, at that moment that this argument is happening, there is very little that can be done about the money that isn't there anyway. And it is always the little things that seem to tear at a person's relationship with his significant other, or best friend. The whole process seemed so important to address and yet what have I learned when I continue in the same stupid procedure again and again with the person I love and value more than anyone else on earth?

Side Note:
At the time this song was written, I had lost the coveted job that

I had with the Parks Department, was again, unemployed, and still finishing up my Computer Sciences degree at SPSCC. Our financial circumstances were dire, but I believe that, because we were full-tithing payers, we were helped from a higher source to make our bills and to get by. I am reminded of a moment during that time where I had very little food in the house and hardly any money. I went to the Tumwater Mega Foods to get some provisions only to find I did not have enough money to get the needed provisional groceries.

As I was going back to my vehicle, out in the parking lot, there was a man who stopped me and told me he was selling potatoes out of the trunk of his car. When he opened his trunk, there was just this one gunny sack of potatoes there.

I was suspicious of the man but after talking to him for a moment, I bought the 100-pound bag of potatoes from him for five dollars. Over the next few weeks till I had a bit more money, we ate mashed and French fried and baked, and, well we did everything to a potato that could be done to them. And to this day, I believe it was a special blessing; maybe even an angel sent to help out the Baldwin family in their time of need.

In The Last

(1989) – In 1987 the Sea-First Bank fell into some hard times, when sister banks in Oklahoma and Texas ran into financial problems. One day three bankers walked into the office of the CEO of JW Electronics and called for their loan to be satisfied, which at the time, was probably over a million dollars. Back then, we thought that there was a good chance that we could, not only find that money through sales of parts and end-products, but that we could remain solvent.

Unfortunately, this was not the case and JW Electronics started going under. Because I was part of the family of the owner, I was called into a special meeting with Diane, her sister Sue and Sue's husband George, Diane's brothers, Jack and Jeff, Diane's sister, Kathy and her husband Ron. A plan was set, promises were made, and hopes were high that we would be able to consolidate things, close down the smaller satellite stores, and come out better than ever.

Of course, this did not happen and things went from bad to worse after the company filed chapter 11 and went through court proceedings to keep the doors open. I think we all punish ourselves for the "might-have-been," or the "should-have," or "could-have," without realizing that what shapes us in life is the learned experiences from mistakes as well as the trials that we go through when things go wrong, as well as the disappointments and sorrows we experience in life.

When this poem was written it was rather evident that JW Electronics was not going to pull out of its financial tailspin and that soon, I would again be unemployed. Off and on I spent 13 years working for a company that, In The Last, would afford me little to nothing. That is to say, at least at the time, all the experience from working there amounted to very little. I had very little retirement benefits due to the fact that they didn't even make it a consideration until the third time I had returned there, and all the promises, all the pie in the sky, all my hopes and aspirations for the future had crumbled beneath my feet.

But I was family, and, regardless of my circumstances or feelings of being handled poorly, family takes care of its own. I knew then that things were going to change and I was going to have to look into other directions for new possibilities.

It was at that moment while looking at where I had come to, from where I had been, that I felt a little empty and cheated after finding out that Ron was purchasing JW Electronics from Jack Weeks to continue with a new name, 'ERI' and had hired most of the staff that was working for JW Electronics, including the other front counter sales people like Steve Terry and Bobby Searl to continue working for Ron;... but in this restructuring, I was not included.

And for all that I had not done under the promise of some future in sales at JW Electronics, that blow hurt the most, but in retrospect, it was probably never meant for me anyway as I went on to get a degree in Computer Sciences at SPSCC.

A Hole In The Sky

(1971) – In 1969, I moved back in with my Grandma Scarbrough while going to Portland State University. It was during this stay that she got a notice from the Oregon State Highway Department, who had decided that there was a need to build a freeway from southeast Vancouver Washington, through the far South East section of Portland and over to Oregon City and then tie that road, which would become Interstate 205, into the main, west coast, north-south Interstate; interstate 5.

Unfortunately, this freeway was routed right through my old neighborhood in Portland where my Grandma Scarbrough lived; the Lents District. There was little negotiation, a lot of legal ups and downs, and inevitably, very poor compensation for the home that Grandma Scarbrough had lived in for over 20 years.

During the negotiations, my dad stopped over to see how I was doing and heard about the travesty. I still remember his response to her when he said, "Jesse James used a gun." The loss of Grandma Scarbrough's house, (which was also at one time, my dad's house), and homestead on 96th Street, just off of Foster Boulevard to the highway department was regrettable to say the least.

Grandma Scarbrough ended up moving to another house about a mile away, but in some respects her spirit and heart were broken from this forced move. Diane and I went to visit her many times in her new home, but she never really settled in, she was never happy or comfortable there, and it was less than two years later that she came down with cancer that metastasized and soon after she quickly passed away.

I wrote this poem to help me deal with the loss of her house, and to help me deal with the loss of my old neighborhood. When I finally went out to the road construction area around the Foster Street neighborhood, the one thing that I noticed at first was the apparent impression of an apocalyptic or Armageddon-like feel in the immediate area.

But then, as I walked down 96th Street, I had to search hard to find exactly where everything used to be. I stood in Leslie's yard staring westward across the street. Gone was what was once a fabulous old home built around the 20s or 30s, gone was the string-bean tree in front and gone was the magnificent ancient black cherry tree in the back yard—but looking out, seeing everything in a state of destruction or just gone, the impression that came to my mind, that I'll never forget was that sense of emptiness; just a hole in the sky.

Through the years I have experienced this same sense of loss every time someone in my neighborhood unnecessarily or ridiculously cuts down a tree, and I think, there's another hole in the sky.

Side Note:

This is one of those songs that I wrote right after I got my first guitar. It is interesting, (I'm rather amazed), that I felt impressed, even back then, to document this occurrence, which I've never gotten over. There is another poem, Where Is The Love, that is also about this subject, but approaches it from a different philosophical and musical standpoint and on the 1993 album, New Suits.

Second Side Note:

Grandma Scarbrough's house didn't make the freeway (dog-gone-it), but instead her yard, the property her house was on as well as two adjacent lots became a part of the off ramp for the Interstate 205 Foster Boulevard exit.

Third Side Note:

My brother John, who I have always respected as someone with impeccable music taste, loved this song, and his opinion amplified the value of the song to me in my own belief system.

Gently Sleep Within My Arms Tonight

(1990) – A lullaby to a baby, being rocked in hopes of peaceful and good, sweet dreams, this poem was written right after Allison Jane was born and I believed her to be my last child. We had a rocking chair in our bedroom that also served as a place where Diane would fall asleep at night while nursing and rocking the baby.

It was my job, well, my pleasure to spend time holding that baby and rocking her whenever I got the chance. By this time, in the fall of

1990, JW Electronics had closed its doors. I was unemployed and going to school at South Puget Sound Community College and taking up Computer Science classes.

This poem was kind of a lullaby that I wrote for her in a medieval setting and fairy tale atmosphere. The tune came to me one evening while I was rocking Allison to sleep. It sounded so good that I felt it would be a wonderful song, but either that funky keyboard of Martha's didn't give me an adequate backup representation, I didn't capture the essence of what I was trying to say and feel with this song, or the translation from performance to recording didn't jell.

I can't say that I was totally disappointed with the results but I was hoping for something else and maybe I will rerecord it at another time and really get that song out.

The Morning March Of The Miniature Mechanical Metal Men

Cousin Martha had the largest collection of 60s and 70s music on records and CDs that I have ever seen,... so, she willingly became my go to person when it came to getting her to record cassettes for me. I was over at her house so much that I think it made her husband nervous.

One day I was over there and playing with their, **Casio CTK520L keyboard** and Martha told me her boys never played it and let me borrow it.

Side Note:

I think this was one of the last recordings I did using Martha's wonderful, **Casio CTK520L keyboard**. There were a couple of other songs and musical ideas, that were recorded towards the end there, including things that are part of the instrumentation albums, **"Somewhere In My**

Life" and, "**No Words Tonight.**" Meanwhile, I had had this keyboard for about two months before Martha's husband Craig wanted it back, and it left my possession in late April.

Another Side Note:

I think I learned a lot by experimenting with the varied sounds and voices and musical ideas the keyboard had to offer and the longer I had it in my possession the more I got to feel the possibilities and options I might take to go in new directions.

It still amazes me that I could take that toy keyboard and do so much with it, and to know there was a lot of possibilities that I never got to experience, still I was able to embellish four and a half albums of engineered recordings.

This is probably a good time and place to thank Martha and Craig for the loan of their keyboard; it served my purposes very well.

119

09 - SPINNING MY WHEELS - 1992

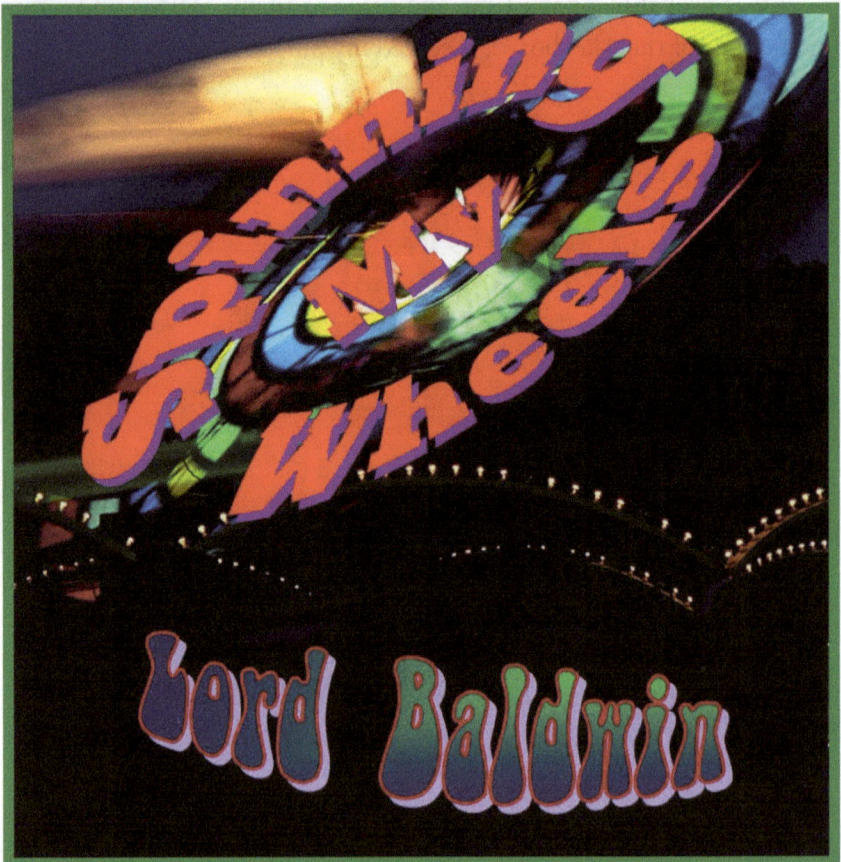

120

꧁꧂

NOTES ABOUT THE
COVERS

By this time I had started trying to create art while making an album cover. I started with a carnival theme and a Ferris wheel tiled as to have each letter to the, Spinning My Wheels, circle,... There's a flame coming out of the circle, giving the illusion that the wheel is un-anchored and it's in motion, being shot into space,... heading out swiftly below are the original covers,... see what you think.

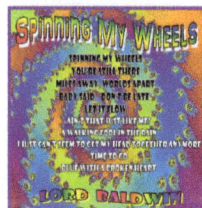

121

SPINNING MY WHEELS

Spinning My Wheels
You're Still There
Miles Away, Worlds Apart
Baby Said, "Don't Be Late"
Let It Flow
Ain't That Just Like Me?
A Walking Fool In The Rain
I Just Can't Seem To Get My Head Together Anymore
Time To Go
Blue With A Broken Heart

122

Spinning My Wheels

High school was a drag, all my teachers just a nag,
it's no wonder I couldn't wait to jump the fence.
Thought I had a solid plan so I left my home and ran
and I've been running on this treadmill ever since.
I been going it alone with these muscles of my own,
I'm compromising my own true ideals.
Though my pals all envy me, because I'm going places and doing things,
they can't see that I'm just spinning my wheels.
Spinning my wheels, pouring on the gas.
Tearing up the road, going nowhere fast.
Without a course of action, I'm just like the flimflam man without a deal.
Tearing up the field like I'm racing down hill,
but I know I'm just standing still.
who am I kidding, I'm just spinning my wheels.
Moved from one place to the next, trying to keep me out of debt,
Too bad I never worked out my own designs.
Working at this nowhere job, and for the money I've been robbed
Without a future I'm just wasting all my time.

Hard to say what might have been if I would have known back then
but now regrets and disappointments are all I feel.
Instead of confidence and wealth and feeling good about myself,
I'm just grinding on and spinning my wheels.
Spinning my wheels, pouring on the gas.
Burning up the road, going nowhere fast.
Hard to differentiate between the fantasy and the real.
Tearing up the field like I'm racing down hill,
but I know I'm just standing still.
who am I kidding, I'm just spinning my wheels.
Spinning my wheels, pouring on the gas.
up the road, going nowhere fast.
Without a course of action, I'm just like the flimflam man without
a deal.
Tearing up the field like I'm racing down hill,
but I know I'm just standing still.
who am I kidding, I'm just spinning my wheels.

123

※

You're Still There

Did you think when you cleaned out
all your stuff from the home,
that I'd stop thinking of you, leaving well enough alone?
Maybe I'd just go search
and find somebody else.
You might think because you're gone that I'm home by myself.
but you're still there in my thoughts, in my prayers and my life.
Though you've gone,
I still hold on to the things we used to share.
You're still there in my heart, in my dreams every night.
Though you've gone and we're apart,
still in heart you're still there.
You couldn't wait any longer
for me to make us a life.
So tired of empty promises that I'd make you my wife.
You're probably thinking
I've washed my hands and we're through.
Or maybe you believe I could be over you,
but you're still there in my thoughts, in my prayers, in my life.
Although you've gone,

I still hold on to the things we used to share.
You're still there in my heart, in my dreams every night.
Though you've gone and we're apart,
still in heart you're still there.

124

Miles Away, Worlds Apart

Miles away, worlds apart. Me on earth, you on the moon.
Hoping there might be a chance,
for us to get together soon.
But with so much between us, how could we hope to start?
Scenes from far-off windows,
miles away, worlds apart.
Caught between your station and my family's class.
Lost between the cold indifference
that I know won't pass.
Pretending there's an equality, to do or say something smart.
But distances don't ever change,
we're miles away, worlds apart.
What foolish games to play as we walk the avenue.
From casual words and implied things
to think you love me too.
My worse dream turned to nightmare
is that I can't touch your heart.
As you go your way and I go mine
We're miles away, worlds apart.

125

Baby Said, "Don't Be Late"

Baby said, "Don't be late," or no food will be on your plate.
She says She just won't wait, and I'll be alone.
I can't blame Her the way she's right;
I been home late every night.
My jobs' been keeping me tight and away from home.
But how can I think with my life in the rough?
With all that I do, I still don't make enough.
I'm sitting here with these bills,
piled high, and I got the chills to match my cough.
I come home with a terrible head, and send everyone to bed,
so I can work instead with worries to think of.
Baby knows of her rights, She turns off all the lights,
calls time out with our fights to bring me love.
Everything just fades away without sound,
all I can think of is this good lady I've found,
who knows I need a break,
and without her I'd never take any time off.

126

Let It Flow

Come on Babe, give it up. This is no way to show love.
How can we flow with the course, if affection must be forced?
Giving up what's right for you, to make sure I'm happy too.
You sacrifice your very need, trying too hard to please me.
Come on Sweetheart, let it flow,
Bring out those lies and let them go.
Though love was lost into the night, we can still salvage it tonight.
You're not here to play a role. Come on Sweetheart, let it flow.
Come on Babe, don't give up.
There's more than one way to be loved.
All we need is just the spark, to be strong here in the dark.
Sharing all that's right for us, and grow from everything that was.
We have our whole lives to think of, lets not try too hard to be
loved.
Come on Sweetheart, let it flow, get out those lies and let them go.
Though love was lost into the night, we can still salvage it tonight.
You're not here to play a role. Come on Sweetheart, let it flow.

127

Ain't That Just Like Me

I've heard it said people will only believe
things they truly want to believe.
And if love is blind, I could never see you,
as anything else but the dream of us two.
So is it so bad that I acted the jerk,
because I wanted so much for this thing to work?
But like a horse with blinders in a happy gait
I kept on going till it was far too late.
Ain't that just like me to carry on, and hold on to a love long gone.
Living the lie while you're so out of range,
and thinking that somehow things will change.
Ain't that just like me, to have so much at the start,
and end up with nothing but a broken heart.
So, I'm sitting here alone, you'd think that I would learn
that my positive attitude, won't make you return.
But I got no regrets, and without faith I would fall,
and I'd have a harder time getting through this all.
So is it so bad that I'd be singing this tune,
that I strive for the best and shoot for the moon?
There's nothing to lose but my own self esteem

to keep looking for you to come back in my dream.
Ain't it just like me to carry on, and hold on to a love long gone.
Living the lie while you're so out of range,
and thinking that somehow things will change.
Ain't it just like me, to have so much at the start,
and end up with nothing but a broken heart.

128

A Walking Fool In The Rain

Shuffling my feet and I'm walking slow,
I got no place to come or go.
Rolling gray clouds hovering while I'm here thinking of Jane,
a walking fool in the rain.
Got back my ring in a foolish fight,
I been on the bum ever since that night.
Rambling aimlessly, looking for her again,
a walking fool in the rain.
A warm breeze blowing drizzle down in waves,
as the northwest summer rain falls quickly in the bay.
Then, all at once it stops, clear waters fill the fountains.
Winds rush the clouds over evergreen mountains.
I got no job, but I'm getting by.
Got lots of plans but all of them seem to die.
Nighttime falling and I got no place to stay,
a walking fool in the rain.
I shouldn't pretend I'm so happy while living this love-sick pain.
A walking fool, you know, Honey,
I'm a walking fool, oh,
a walking fool in the rain.

129

I Just Can't Seem To Get My Head Together Anymore

I just can't seem to get my head together anymore,
it lies on distant shores with no purpose anymore.
And though I try so hard to think like I did before,
I must have burned out,
oh, must have burned out,
burned out to the core.

I just cant seem to get my friends together anymore,
they all hang down at the store, crashed out on the floor.
Dying in a basement that is crumbling with the times,
they must have burned out,
oh, they must have burned out,
burned clear out of their minds.

Sometimes, you think it's the end,
At times, I know, you might need a friend,
and help is just beyond your quick belief.

But just when you thought you'd be,
it didn't really want to leave
and the weaker minds found no relief.
I just don't see no future here, with no one left to meet,
it's up some one-way street getting closer to the heat.
If going back is hard, my Lord, it's the only way it seems,
I've got to get back,
oh, I've got to get back,
all my charcoal dreams.

130

Time To Go

Things were so easy when all he needed was love.
Life was so simple with everything taken care of.
He looks round the farm for a comfort or something to hold.
He looks down the hills to the streets of the city below.

A burning within drives him crazy toward the big need.
He knows he must do this alone to truly succeed.
The dreams he now holds are all abstract and strain to flow.
He doesn't know why something whispers, "It's time to go."

From a window she follows the son who would soon wander free.
Unlike his confusion, she knows what is destined to be.
That pain of tomorrow burns deep, like being alone.
She knew that someday he would need to be out on his own.

The migration of youth, he will journey far from today.
Yet first he must leave the safe nest and fly away.
How she'll live here without his presence, she doesn't know.
With no self-deception, she understands it's time to go.

The father feels the changes like everyone else.
The boy who would be man, so much like himself.
The need to go out to proclaim individual might.
The need to decide for himself what is wrong and is right.

From bikes to Scouting, to sports, to cars, and to girls;
and from relating to family to striking out in the real world.
With a smile his Dad tries not to let his broken heart show,
but instead with support, gives his hand, as it's time to go.

131

Blue With A Broken Heart

I'm blue with a broken heart; all my music ain't got no spark.
I pine for you every night past dark,
and I'm blue with a broken heart.

I tried to ask you not to go to Carolyn,
Those Charlotte men look so dandy and fine.
With deceiving ways, always up to no good.
Making me look like I'm just a hick from the woods.

And I'm blue with a broken heart,
all my music ain't got no spark.
I pine for you every night past dark,
and I'm blue with a broken heart.

I'm still entertaining every night at John's
but no one dances without you singing my songs.
You know, the gangs' been kind, but then they got no choice,
they miss *you* Honey, and your angel voice.

And we're all blue with a broken heart,

all my music ain't got no spark.
I pine for you every night past dark,
and I'm blue with a broken heart.

My letter left here on the five-oh-two,
but I ain't sure it's going to get to you.
I want you to know, I don't care where you've been,
I just want you back home with me again.

Till then I'll be blue with a broken heart,
all my music ain't got no spark.
I pine for you every night past dark,
and I'm blue with a broken heart.

I32

꧁꧂

MEMOIRS & NOTES - 09 -
'SPINNING MY WHEELS'

Spinning My Wheels

(1979-80) – In 1979-80, this poem was born from retrospectively looking back at all the different directions and dead-ends that I experienced. It was on my list and slated to be the Number "2" song recorded at Stoney's recording studio in 1985, but because of the great and terrible theft, that never happened.

At the time that I wrote this poem; looking at my life and realizing that without a plan or direction, I'm just *spinning my wheels*, I really was *Spinning My Wheels*, in fact, I felt that, temporally and vocationally, I had little direction and purpose in life, and going with the flow of however things turned out.

But at the time, perhaps I didn't view things quite the same as I should have. I had a good family thing going on, with a loving wife and best friend, four kids; one boy and three girls, and aside from not being accomplished in my professional career, I was a relatively happy guy.

And, it's been my experience that I have always been looking forward to how things will be or might be someday in the future, without analyzing or realizing how good things were at that time in my life. Maybe I thought I had a plan but seeing that that plan didn't work out or maybe needed a little more thought to make it come to work, I was distraught.

This kind of thing is what complicates people's lives, but arguably, part of the learning process in life most of us experience as we are just passing through. Perhaps this song is one of the best songs I wrote during my slump period, but it epitomized the frustration and realization that without education and/or planning for one's future, a person can pretty much expect that they'll never progress or climb out, and inevitably, they'll have to take what they get.

Side Note:
More than half of the songs in this album, *"Spinning My Wheels,"* as well as almost all of the songs in the next album, "Heaven," were embellished and recorded with the new **Yamaha PRS-500 keyboard.** This song and a few other songs were good songs but did not make it on any of the earlier albums due to certain timing constraints. Also, I wanted to rerecord, "Spinning My Wheels," with the new keyboard and embellish it with some of the new percussion and cool, new backup sounds.

As I put this album together, I felt that the time spent and the esoteric nature of the deep-seated recording, as well as the general feel of the song, everything combined was just too close to what I wanted the end product to be to instead, cast off into my musical bone yard. So much so, that I not only kept it just the way it was, but it became the foreshadowed, underlying theme of and namesake for this album.

You're Still There

(1991) – During my prolific writing period while working at the Washington State Parks and Recreation, I let any and all emotional psychological and spiritual feelings that came to me become a consideration for a poem. Lost love and the ramifications of realizing that it was a mistake to let that person go.

One day, out of the blue I got this call from Daryl, who I hadn't heard from for a couple of years. He told me that his girlfriend had left him and although she was gone, it was like her ghost or her essence permeated the walls and the rooms and, he felt it was like she had never left or that she would return at any moment. He was really depressed to the point that he was considering doing something drastic or stupid, like suicide.

I told him to hold on and I would be over at his place as soon as I got off work. I drove over to the house that he was renting at the time and went up to the front door and rang the doorbell that made no sound and perhaps didn't work. After I knocked loudly, the bark of a huge St. Bernard reverberated the living room, (after being bitten in my youth, (seven) I have a fear of and ultimately, don't do dogs), but no one came to answer the door. I began to look into all the open windows I could, to see if he was in the house, but I found no one.

His flat-black Land Cruiser was not parked outside, so after I confirmed the garage was empty, I was not too worried and I went back into my car, pulled out my guitar, and wrote this song. After a while, Daryl came back from the store and stood outside my car listening, but I was so engrossed composing the words that I didn't realize he was even there. When he found out that I wrote this song for him and about him, he was again impressed and honored, but even better, he was again in better spirits.

I called home to let Diane know where I was and what I was doing and stayed with Daryl till late that night, but I was not thoroughly convinced that he would not do something irrational, so I had him follow me back over to my house. We both got a good, late makeshift dinner from Diane, and then, after I played music till 4 AM, we both went to sleep. I got up the next morning to go to work and left him sleeping on my couch.

When I came back home that evening, he was gone. I was still worried so I tried to call him up over at his place but I just got an answering machine. After work, I drove over to his house and found that his vehicle was there. Also, there was music playing inside, but no one answered the door except the big dog that was outside and he followed me around as I went from window to window looking through to see if and where he was in there.

After a thorough search I realized that he was not at home, and so, once again I camped out there in his driveway and waited for him to return. Around 11 PM, he finally pulled in and got out of another vehicle, moving with a drunken stagger. He was very happy to see me. A couple of seconds later a girl exited from the other side of the other vehicle and thus, the crisis was over.

I continued to call him every day for about two weeks until he got too busy doing his other things; often he was never at home and he never returned my phone calls. Eventually I lost contact with Daryl and didn't hear from him again for another three years.

Miles Away, Worlds Apart

(1991) – At one of the church dances in the winter of 1990, my daughter, Lori, who was a sophomore in high school, met this boy, Chris, through her good friend Christi Gardener. Lori alluded to the fact that they were kind of seeing each other, but from the many hours spent on the phone and her obsession with going to all the stake dances and activities, I kind of knew that there was something more.

Chris's family lived in Lacey in one of the more exclusive areas for people with more affluent lifestyles and they were strong LDS church members. After a few other dates, that is to say, dates not involving church activities, they were unofficially going together and they became an item.

When I went to pick Lori up from a dance one Saturday night,

Christi gleefully ran up to me and told me in front of Lori, who was by now embarrassed, that Lori and Chris were officially going steady.

As summer arrived, Chris began to include Lori more and more into many of his family's activities and outings, including trips to the science center, going out to sporting events and fashionable restaurants, or going on small trips and water-skiing with their $25,000.00 Nautique ski boat. (that's $25,000.00 in 1990).

But unfortunately, there was trouble in paradise that at first was only perceived but later became more evident. I had never met Chris's parents, but I did talk to them on the phone a couple of times. I thought it was neat that Lori could have a boyfriend whose parents were well off, especially because they were members of the LDS church, which, I thought, or wrongfully assumed, was supposed to level the playing field a bit.

But being the party on the lower-class level in a love relationship, it was soon evident that the, happy-ever-after possibilities were doomed. I became aware of a problem after Lori returned with little innuendoes or hints in passing. At first it was kind of a joking implication that because we lived in a low-income housing area called Evergreen Shores, and because I was one of the unfortunate people who at the time was unemployed, Lori was from the "other" side of the tracks. Then after an extended trip with them to Lake Chelan where a lot of questions were asked of Lori and information gathered about me and my family circumstances, mostly by Chris's father, there was a decided mood change and, after talking with them, I came away with a sense of unapproachable aloofness that rapidly turned into a kind of cold, unfriendly, standoffish overtone.

And of course, with my innocence, (or ignorance) to the matters, I thought that it was just me, after all, I am a rather enigmatic person to most people that don't know me. Although Lori continued to report little things about their supposed collective mannerisms and attitudes, I still fell back on my belief that they were good people because they were, after all, in the church and so, were probably just goofing on her, like I might if I was in the same circumstances.

But later, the allusion of suggestions or negative hints became more real as things were not only mentioned or insinuated to Lori, but suggestions were made that maybe she didn't really like Chris after all, and maybe she should find another person, herself. Then Lori found out from Chris that his parents didn't think Lori was the right kind of person for him and that he should break up with her and find someone more suitable.

There was some kidding around to Chris by his father, who implied or hinted that one of his golf friends down the street had a daughter that would be perfect for Chris, but it all seemed so staged and put on that Chris and Lori dismissed it. But to me, this developing plot seemed similar to that of the 1984 film, *the Karate Kid* and I was now concerned.

For a short while Chris ignored the admonitions of his parents and continued to see Lori who was as confused as Diane and I about the whole thing, but we let it ride, still thinking it was some kind of head game at worst and that they would come around. After a couple of weeks passed, we not only didn't see Chris coming over, or hear from him calling all the time like before, but Lori, who was suddenly downhearted and real moody, was purposely missing the Stake Center church dances and she was avoiding her friends in Lacey, including her best friend, Christi Gardner.

One night after seeing Lori decidedly upset in her room, I brought up the subject to Diane who quietly informed me that Lori had informed her that Lori and Chris had broken up. The story followed that Lori, who was having me drive her to the dances again in spite of knowing full well that Chris's parents didn't want their son to be involved with her anymore, went to a dance and waited in the foyer for Chris to arrive. After about an hour had passed, Chris finally pulled up in a sports car and walked in smiling from ear to ear, escorted by another girl; and yes, it was that other girl that lived down the street and whose parents were friends with Chris's folks.

Later I heard the rest of the story from my son Chet, who told me that after Chris's parents had unsuccessfully tried to break them up,

Chris's father told Chris that if Chris finally broke up with Lori, Chris's father would buy his son a Datsun 300ZX sports car.

It had to have been all just too much for a 17-year-old kid who, in his defining moment, instead of proving himself to his true love, found out that he had his price and got bought off.

This incident not only broke Lori's heart, but ours as well. I wrote the words for this poem for Lori who would cry listening to it at first and then moved on into college and so, moved on in her life.

Side Note:

After getting the job with the Washington State Parks Department, there was a lot of going back and forth from the college to the trailer/modular unit/temp that housed the facilities. It was about three blocks away from the Tumwater High School so there were times that I would drop off Lori and Chet at school or pick them up and take them home before I headed back to the college to take night classes and or do homework.

And it was around this time that Lori already had her driver's license and was driving around "**the Green Pickle**" and, I guess I should have figured that the 17-foot long, seven-foot wide, eight-foot high, the ugly **"Green Pickle"** probably did not check off very many of the boxes that a teenage girl in high school might have.

And sure enough, one day Lori convinced me that she needed to learn how to drive a stick. Now I'd already faced certain death teaching her how to drive and now she wanted to start all over again with my **67 Chevy Nova**? Really? The first time was hard enough, but now, for what it was worth, she had a license that said she was ready to take on any vehicle in the world.

My fears were put into actions as she approached driving the **67 Chevy** saying that she'd practiced with someone else's car and knew all about it, but after she didn't put in the clutch right and the gears were grinding underneath me, I told her that different vehicles have different clutches that feel and work differently.

After a painful reentry into that world of scenarios like, "No I didn't", or, "Yes I did," and, "It's not my fault," and, "I did what you said to do," and after a painful two weeks, (Lori was relentless when she wanted to be), she got the hang of it.

And Lord knows I should have know what would be next. It happened at about three in the afternoon. I was working at my cubicle at the Parks Department when Lori showed up and wanted to borrow the car. I told her that I needed the car to get home myself but she assured me she would be back by then.

As we walked outside to where the Chevy was parked, I was telling her all about the idiosyncrasies of the car and she nodded and nodded, but I'm sure she heard nothing. And it was really a strange, almost surreal thing to see the taillights of that **67 Chevy Nova** illuminate; that same car that I had towed up to Washington State from Molalla Oregon and rebuilt the engine and drive train with Gary Rook in the garage of the Funeral home,... and to watch my car as my daughter drove it away,... not sure why, but it was really a strange sight that has stayed with me to this day.

Baby Said, "Don't Be Late"

(1976) – This is another one of those songs that sounds great live but something was lost in the translation when it was recorded. I'm thinking, maybe if I tried a different sound, rhythm or tempo, I don't know, something.

Those lean times where we spend a lot of time and energy chasing after rainbows only to find the clouds rolling back in and the rain falling hard. I wrote this just after Chet was born and I was involved with a couple of get-rich schemes like the Amway and Shacklee network marketing industries, you know? All of them promising pie in the sky, but in fact, demand all of your time and energy after you've gotten home from work, and all you want to do is hang out with your family.

Well, I tried them all, and they're all the same; someone else somewhere else on the elusive pyramid is getting richer every time I bring someone new to the organization. I don't think we ever profited from the sales part of the scheme, and I don't know why, but it seemed like everybody I brought in seemed to fizzle out (or wise up), leaving my part of the pyramid and me without any foundation.

Anyway, I am gone away on Tuesday nights, Wednesday nights, Thursday nights and some Friday nights, not to mention that occasional regional meeting up in Tacoma on Saturday nights, while Diane is stuck at home with two babies and ultimately, because of the incoming costs and transportation, I end up with no extra money. So, I wrote this poem to reflect the many times that I came home late to find Diane and the kids already gone to bed and asleep, while I ultimately accomplished little to nothing anyway.

Fortunately for me, Diane not only understood, but supported me in the fruitless pursuits of a better way. This all came to an end one night when I came home late and she was not asleep. And she asked, "Is this working for us?" I said, "Not really." And she asked, "Is this really what you want to do?" And I answered, "No." And, thank goodness, that was the end of it.

Let It Flow

(1991) –Diane and I have good communication skills and we know each other pretty well. It was not always this way. Working on and dealing with our need for better communication and verbal correspondence skills was always a bit of a challenge, especially because I felt the need to feed my ego and to be right. This poem is about that realization that being right is rarely the right path to a loving relationship. In 1978, our Prophet, Spencer W. Kimball published a book titled, "Marriage." In that book it stated that the biggest reason people get divorced is because they get selfish and stop trying to communicate with each other and therefore stop trying to work their problems out. Also, he suggested that we stop and listen to what the other has to say before selfishly driving home our own point of view. I took a lot of that council very seriously and tried to remember to exercise those principals whenever we'd get in a tiff. But sorry to say, I'm not perfect and don't always follow the directions offered by the Prophet, and we did continue to have confusing and uncomfortable moments where my listening skills were less than perfect and our relationship was tested. This poem was about some of those conversations turned to arguments and about our ongoing inabilities to deal with our financial ineptitudes.

We had many times where one or both of us just gave up or gave in to the unfortunate or stilted circumstances, and how we failed to exchange the right few words that could have diverted the grief and misunderstanding in our own personal lives and in our home. But we never gave up on each other and we learned about the miracle of forgiveness. Over time, we have gotten better in our communication skills. This poem was about a look at the other's perspective. This poem was also about that hope to do better; to be better for each other.

Ain't That Just Like Me

(1991) – When the church ward boundaries were split, our family and the people around us in our neighborhood ended up combining with half of another ward. One of my new friends was a guy named Ray Matthews, who listened to and was excited by my original material.

We got together many times and worked out some of his musical ideas along with mine. We did a lot of pseudo-performances together and I was surprised at how well we worked together, considering the fact that neither one of us knew the other very well. After a performance at the church one Saturday night, Ray was hot, I mean to say he could do no wrong, so we went over to his house and jammed till after one.

We did a lot of original material and stuff out of our heads, impromptu stuff that sounded pretty good.

One of the songs that came out after dinking around with chords was this song which, until he left for Utah in 1995, was one of the songs that we played together. I talked with Ray a couple of times after that but over the years and the distance between I've lost whatever relationship we had. But at one time, we had it right there.

A Walking Fool In The Rain

(1991) – During the last six months of 1973 and the first nine months of 1974, I worked as a sub-contractor, doing concrete flatwork and in between jobs, I was painting houses. In the fall of that year, Diane and I moved from Portland up to Kelso and I started to work at the JW Electronics store in Longview. That move did not pan out too well, because the store manager, Ben was feeling threatened by already having the owner's son working there, and then now me, a son-in-law coming in to get trained; looking like if I stayed for any length of time, he might just be the odd man out. So after a short stint there, Ben convinced the owner that I wasn't working out too well, and I was transferred up to the main store in Olympia.

After arriving in Olympia our financial circumstances were rather bleak, so I put ads in the newspapers soliciting my possible services as a painter and concrete worker. I ended up painting a lot of houses, and I did a little bit of concrete work, but it seemed that the Pacific Northwest, being particularly wet, did not present as many opportunities for outside work in the winter, so I stuck with interior and exterior house painting. We had a car; it was Grandma Scarbrough's 1959 Chevy Belfair, a big wide metal car with the big horizontal fins. Not a real reliable car and at the time, a gas guzzler, so, because we lived in town at the time, I found myself walking to most of these particular painting jobs.

It was on one of these occasions, I was walking down Puget Street past the church, walking to this particular job to paint a house with oil-based paint, when it started raining. A thought came to me, and I imagined myself with no car, no home to speak of, and there I am, walking in the rain. The scenario was altered as words came to my mind and I thought of a person whose single purpose is to find his lost girlfriend. Thus, everything in his life is lost, including his love and he figures that the only way that he can put his life back together is to find that girl; that one person that he was engaged to or married to, and he's out there looking for Jane. The tune danced in my mind as the lyrics all fit into place, and although I didn't make it home until after 1130 that night, I stayed up, wrote all the lyrics, pounded out the chords on the guitar and thus, 'A Walking Fool In The Rain' was created.

I Just Can't Seem To Get My Head Together Anymore

(1969-71) – I left Reno Nevada at the end of summer in 1969 after my relationship with my once girlfriend, Mary Homer had broken up with me and afterwards, fallen completely apart and I headed back to Portland Oregon to start college at Portland State University. This was, for no other reason but to stay out of Vietnam and the draft. The whole relationship thing had left a bad taste my mouth and I decided that on the way home I would take a detour, a rather extensive detour to my old stomping grounds in Glendora California, which is in the foothills of Los Angeles.

It had been two years since I was back there and I was going to look up the old gang and see how things were going. I envisioned having a terrific time with my friends before I started back in school. I never expected that I would be finding most of my friends in a whole different circumstance. A lot of guys that I used to hang out with had left Glendora, and some of them, California altogether. Some of my friends were in jail with indeterminable terms for reasons unknown. Some of my friends were away on vacations of their own, due to the fact that it was the end of the summer.

A couple of my friends had gotten drafted and were in Vietnam. There were four main people that I wanted to see but none of them were there and I was forced to settle for my secondary or passing friends. The worse thing was, most of my friends in passing still around were now into a whole different thing then I was ever into. I was never into hard drugs; especially shooting-up drugs, (never liked even seeing people do this), and I was appalled and ultimately or immediately alienated by them, their actions and frankly, the whole process.

One of the last places I visited had some of my friends holed up in a small motel room that had cardboard covering up the windows; my friends (and others not too happy that I was even there), were all lying around on the floors, completely zoned-out and stoned to the Max.

I was scared just being in the room or being around the Seconal and the cocaine, but to be sure, I was really uneasy with the heroin scene. I felt very anxious and uncomfortable with this whole new, weird scene, and felt it could get out of hand at any moment,... and I knew I needed to get out of there and as quickly as possible. And because my close friends and people that I remembered weren't even there, I left.

So after only being there one day, I got back out on the freeway in the early afternoon, put my thumb out and hitchhiked up interstate five to head back for Oregon. I arrived somewhere about 16 hours later at my dad's farm (about 2:30 in the morning) and then went out to the barn and was sleeping in the hayloft till my dad woke me up when he went out to the barn to milk the cows and do the chores.

Time To Go

(1989) – Although the words to this poem was written in 1989 and my children did not start leaving home until 1992, I envisioned not only the perspective of myself, the parent, I was looking at the point of view of the child (like when I was out of high school) that was growing up and would be leaving his or her home to progress onward. I tried to address perspectives from a mother's love and concern and from her viewpoint as well as from the father's love and respect for this evolutionary process.

Just a couple months before I graduated from high school, I was in the back pasture of the farm, standing up on a hill by the small group of trees close to the railroad tracks, thinking that this is all going to end soon, and all the comfort and the security of living there on the farm was ultimately going to end, and I was going to have to find a new direction and purpose in my life. And I was kind of scared because I knew I had not prepared myself for this inevitability; and I didn't have much time to do it. Sure, I had already lived on my own in upstate New York and New York City, but I knew that I always had somewhere to go; a place to be, to return to, like my mother's home or my dad's farm. But this next move would be a game changer. I would always be welcome in my mother's place or my dad's farm, but I would never be living there again. I would need to find my own way out there in the real world. I knew on that day that when I finally left the farm, there was no place to return to and I would be on my own.

Blue With A Broken Heart

(1984) – At the time this song was written I was so productive in my song creations that I was even getting songs in my dreams.

And so it was with this song; I found myself in the back hills of Tennessee sitting on a big rock, barefooted, wearing a pair of farmer jeans and a tee shirt, playing guitar and singing, *Blue With A Broken Heart*. An eclectic but enthusiastic audience had gathered; a collection of what looked to be farmers and their wives, various hillbillies, kids, down-home folks, ragged, barefooted, but genuinely interested and being entertained with me singing my songs.

An older woman looking kind of like Minnie Pearl, stepped up and said she was friends with someone that knew someone that worked in the back of the stage at the Grand Ole Opry and she made arrangements for me to be invited to play there.

Next thing I knew, I was up there on the stage and I was belting out *Blue With A Broken Heart*, again, and it was a hit. Before I knew what was happening, I was backstage signing a contract and a recording deal, and,... I remember that for me, at that time, life was good.

And then I woke up, and had to go to work. On the way to the funeral home, I penciled out most of the lyrics as I remembered them to be, on the dashboard of my 66 Plymouth Fury III station wagon.

When I got to the funeral home, business was kind of dead, so I went into the casket room, grabbed my beater guitar that I had stashed in the Cherrywood casket and then re-familiarized myself with the tune.

That evening when I came home, I was excited to play the tune to Diane, who has always been a good barometer for my material, so imagine my disappointment when I found her to be less than enthusiastic about the song. As I remember, she said something like, "Well it's okay, I mean,..." Which to me meant, it had little to no substance and was therefore a dud.

I put the song away, only returning to the song briefly to see if I should rework the lyrics or the music, but I did neither. Fast-forward a couple of *months* later, my daughter Meridith, who was five at the time, was walking around the house singing the chorus to, *Blue With A Broken Heart* and I then realized that, *Blue With A Broken Heart* had much more potential then I envisioned.

I grabbed my guitar and then sang the song again to Diane, who smiled enthusiastically and said, "Wow. That's a really good song."

And thus, *Blue With A Broken Heart* has become a family staple and if Meridith is around, she will take the lead and sing the song. It is always a crowd favorite when performed in public.

133

NOTES ABOUT THE
AUTHOR AND BOOK ONE

Lord Baldwin;

Playwright, Songwriter, Keyboardist, Guitarist, Singer/Performer and Jazz Harmonica Player. Emerging from the 60s rock era, has developed a distinctive and rather eclectic style that blends blues, jazz, folk and rock.

In 1983, Lord Baldwin had a renaissance and revitalization to his songwriting and performing and from a renewed perspective and sense of value, after reevaluating priorities, realizing the blessings and strengths of his family and friends, his own special style began to surface; through his poetry and music he documented his life and times.

As new songs began to flow, (even from within his dreams), Lord Baldwin documented the words, (poetry-lyrics), while they were fresh in his mind and he mentally documented the music that would eventually accompany the lyrics.

In 1989 or was it 1990, Lord Baldwin purchased a 4-track, Tascam Cassette Recorder, and immediately began to record. He then took the songs and engineered them into albums, each 45 minutes, so as to fill each side of a 90-minute cassette.

From that simple beginning, Lord Baldwin continued his analog recordings for the next ten years (1991 to 2001), into what has come to be known as, "**The Archive Series**" which is comprised of thirty-eight albums as well as six experimentation instrumentals and other compositions.

This here is the first book of Lord Baldwin's anthological works; '**From The Lost Letters Sent – Book ONE: 1985 - 1992 Memoirs From An Invisible Songwriter**',... Documenting the lyrics and memoirs of songs, musical compositions and stories from his **first nine albums**; documenting the **ninety-two songs** that were recorded between April of 1985 and July of 1992, where Lord Baldwin plays guitars, keyboards, pianos, harmonicas and all the other instruments as well as supplying all the voices to the recordings.

For the curious follower of Lord Baldwin music, this book can be also used as a companion while he or she examines an album, (presently streaming worldwide), they can also gain insightful stories that may accompany the songs they are listening to, and be able to read the lyrics as well as.

Lord Baldwin's heart-felt thanks go out to you for your interest and he wishes you well as you embark on this epic new journey.

Index by Name of Song

MORE BOOKS BY
LORD CHESTER L. BALDWIN II

From The Lost Letters Sent - *Memoirs Of An Invisible Songwriter*
Book ONE: 1985 – 1992

From The Lost Letters Sent - *Memoirs Of An Invisible Songwriter*
Book TWO: 1992 – 1993

From The Lost Letters Sent - Memoirs Of An Invisible Songwriter
Book THREE: 1993 – 1994

From The Lost Letters Sent - Memoirs Of An Invisible Songwriter
Book FOUR: 1995 – 2001

Stepping Between The Ants – Book ONE: *The Winter Escape*

Stepping Between The Ants – Book TWO: *The Spring Ahead*

Stepping Between The Ants – Book THREE: *A Summer To Remember*

Stepping Between The Ants – Book FOUR: *The Fall Behind*

RESILIENT: A (Web-Based Episodic) Musical Play & Story

"'Heads' Or 'Tales From The Summer Of Love'"

www.ingramcontent.com/pod-product-compliance
Lightning Source LLC
Chambersburg PA
CBHW062115020426
42335CB00013B/979